Writing With Style

Writing With Style

APA Style Made Easy

FIFTH EDITION

LENORE T. SZUCHMAN
Barry University

WADSWORTH
CENGAGE Learning

Australia • Brazil • Japan • Korea • Mexico • Singapore • Spain • United Kingdom • United States

WADSWORTH
CENGAGE Learning™

Writing With Style:
APA Style Made Easy,
Fifth Edition
Lenore T. Szuchman

Publisher: Linda Schreiber-Ganster

Executive Editor: Jon-David Hague

Assistant Editor: Rebecca Rosenberg

Editorial Assistant: Kelly Miller

Marketing Manager: Kim Russell

Marketing Assistant: Anna Andersen

Marketing Communications Manager: Talia Wise

Content Project Management: Pre-Press PMG

Creative Director: Rob Hugel

Art Director: Vernon Boes

Print Buyer: Judy Inouye

Rights Acquisitions Account Manager, Text: Bob Kauser

Rights Acquisitions Account Manager, Image: John Hill

Production Service: Pre-Press PMG

Copy Editor: Pre-Press PMG

Cover Designer: Paula Goldstein, Blue Bungalow Design

Cover Image: Harry Briggs

Compositor: Pre-Press PMG

For product information and technology assistance, contact us at **Cengage Learning Customer & Sales Support, 1-800-354-9706.**

For permission to use material from this text or product, submit all requests online at **www.cengage.com/permissions.**

Further permissions questions can be e-mailed to **permissionrequest@cengage.com.**

Library of Congress Control Number: 2009944217

ISBN-13: 978-0-8400-3167-9

ISBN-10: 0-8400-3167-X

Wadsworth
20 Davis Drive
Belmont, CA 94002-3098
USA

Cengage Learning is a leading provider of customized learning solutions with office locations around the globe, including Singapore, the United Kingdom, Australia, Mexico, Brazil, and Japan. Locate your local office at: **www.cengage.com/global.**

Cengage Learning products are represented in Canada by Nelson Education, Ltd.

To learn more about Wadsworth, visit **www.cengage.com/wadsworth**

Purchase any of our products at your local college store or at our preffered online store **www.CengageBrain.com.**

Printed in the United States of America
1 2 3 4 5 6 7 14 13 12 11 10

JUN 2010

For Reuben and Ida

Brief Contents

Contents

C H A P T E R **10**

Grooming Tips for Psychology Papers 126

C H A P T E R **11**

Preparing a Presentation 138

Preface

Writing With Style offers psychology students a new method for learning to write research papers in the style described in the *Publication Manual of the American Psychological Association* (American Psychological Association, 2010). This book calls students' attention to the style of writing used in professional journals and leads them through a process of collecting examples of words, phrases, and sentences that illustrate the essential stylistic components. Students may use these examples in their own papers.

This book can be used in several types of classes. Ideally, it should be used early in the training of psychology majors but after composition requirements have been completed. Moreover, this book may be assigned as the first month's work in a writing-intensive course such as research methods or experimental psychology. It can also be used to replace writing requirements in lower-level content courses such as developmental psychology. In this case, students can be instructed to use only journals related to the content area in their assignments. Those students will be less intimidated by assignments using journal sources in subsequent courses. If a university's program permits, this book can be assigned by the English composition faculty in sections designed for psychology majors.

Many beginning graduate students are also in need of the training this book provides. These students may use this book as a supplement in their first graduate research methods classes or upon entry into the graduate program.

Why It Is Difficult for Students to Master APA Format

American Psychological Association (APA)–style writing is a skill often targeted for study in research methods classes, but psychology students are usually expected to conform to APA guidelines in all of their written work. Sometimes the transition from first-year composition classes to psychology classes leaves students confused because initial composition classes tend to be taught with emphasis on the Modern Language Association (MLA) style. In these courses, students generally learn how to construct a paragraph, how to write a five-paragraph essay, how to develop a thesis statement, and how to write a library research paper in the generic (MLA-based) style. This approach is a useful start, but it does not enhance students' technical writing skills as much as psychology professors would like.

Shortly after declaring a psychology major, students must master a technical writing style that often contradicts the very "laws" they have learned in their composition classes. They must learn to write using APA style, which includes not only rules made explicit in the *Publication Manual*, but also other conventions that constitute the *unwritten* rules of APA style (e.g., rather than writing about what other authors *said* or *believed*, concentrate on what they *found* or *reported*; do not mention the title of someone's article in a literature review; use the passive voice in certain circumstances).

To master this new style, students are usually instructed to purchase the *Publication Manual* or the *Concise Rules of APA Style* (American Psychological Association, 2010) and use it as a reference. However, it is difficult for the student who is new to the style to use the *Publication Manual* or the *Concise Rules* in that way. One reason may be that students have little experience reading material written in APA style at that point in their training. This workbook fills this gap.

Learning by Modeling

Completing the exercises in *Writing With Style* will familiarize students with APA style by a method that helps them begin to *read* APA publications. These exercises require students to scan APA journals for examples of particular rules and conventions. These students then learn by modeling these techniques. The lists generated by completing the exercises in this book will help students when they write their own papers; all the words and phrases contained in these exercises exemplify not only APA style but also the research psychologist's tone and form. Thus, students benefit from the *process* of searching for examples in psychology journals as well as from the *item file* they develop and can use in writing their papers and research reports.

It is daunting for the newly declared psychology major to see the *Publication Manual* and realize that all writing must conform to a style set out in what looks like a reference book rather than a style guide. In fact, the *Publication Manual* is both, but many students need help in figuring out how to use it. For example, there are some rules in the *Publication Manual* that students *must* learn, but others that they do not have to learn. That is, some rules must become second nature (e.g., what tense to use for the method of an experiment), whereas others are used only occasionally and do not have to be memorized (e.g., how to abbreviate a certain measurement). I focus on the rules that should be learned while pointing the way to types of things that should be looked up.

Throughout this book, I call attention to the need for precision in word usage. Students who are new to scientific writing have not always been trained to seek the type of precision required. For example, I point out that when directing readers to consult a figure or a table, it is important to think about what verbs are possible if *table* is the subject of a sentence. Likewise, students should consider what verbs are possible when an *experiment* is the subject—experiments cannot *try* to do anything, for example.

Students should not expect this book to replace the *Publication Manual* or the *Concise Rules*. They should be aware that this is one of several reference books that belong near them when they write. The exercises in *Writing With Style* do not cover every writing situation described in the *Publication Manual* or the *Concise Rules*. After all, most of the information in the *Publication Manual* is not going to be used by any one writer. There is also a suggestion in the *Publication Manual* to consult their web site, http://www.apastyle.org, for the latest information. Here, I provide general descriptions of the desired contents of each section of the research report (something that is covered in the *Publication Manual* but not in the *Concise Rules*), and I give primary emphasis to areas that students often find most difficult. Instructors are likely to find that many of the key points in this book remind them of errors in papers they have graded.

Writing With Style also will not replace a good grammar and punctuation reference. However, I do cover some general rules about both throughout the book, especially in Chapter 10, "Grooming Tips for Psychology Papers," because, in my experience, students often require additional practice with certain basic grammar and punctuation rules. These include how to identify and avoid run-on sentences and how to use a colon. These exercises also require that students scan psychology journals to search for examples of the accurate application of rules.

Content

After Chapter 1, which offers suggestions to students about why and how to use this book, the order of the chapters is flexible. Chapter 2 contains general conventions, such as how to refer to the work of others in the body of a paper and tips for avoiding biased language. This chapter is general enough to have some applicability to any section of a research report.

The sections themselves are covered in Chapters 3 through 9 in the order in which many people write and teach them. It would not be difficult, however, to assign these chapters in some other order. Some might want to assign Chapter 9, or parts of it, very early because of the information on formatting. Chapter 10 contains guidance on avoiding the grammar and punctuation errors that are commonly found in undergraduate psychology papers. This chapter can be assigned at any point in a course, but students seem to find this type of work more useful after they have attempted some writing of their own. The chapter on presentations is last because it is likely to be assigned only if presentations themselves are assigned. Many students will nevertheless benefit from having access to this material whenever they do prepare their first presentations.

The appendix, "Wrapping It Up," contains advice on rewriting. Students often assume that proofreading and revising are the same. I make several specific suggestions here for revising. Then I lead readers through a series of proofreading exercises, directing them to rely on their word processors to spot potential problems. This material is presented as an appendix to encourage instructors to assign it whenever students are preparing their first assigned papers.

Because some students may confuse modeling and plagiarism, in the first chapter, I include an extensive discussion of plagiarism. In addition, after they have worked a few of the exercises, students will understand that many authors use similar constructions; these constructions must therefore be in the public domain. The concept of plagiarism should be clearer in the student's mind after completing this workbook than it was before.

New in the Fifth Edition

I have kept this volume brief so that it can be used as a supplement for a variety of courses. For some courses, it is likely that students will have their own copies of the *Publication Manual* or the *Concise Rules*, but some instructors will find that there is enough material here for students to complete assignments for certain classes without purchasing either of those books.

The most important change is that this edition is based on style rules as expressed in the sixth edition of the *Publication Manual*. Furthermore, the tables at the end of each chapter are now keyed to that edition and to the current edition of the *Concise Rules* as well.

Second, all exercise examples keyed to InfoTrac have been removed. Many students were confused by these examples because InfoTrac had not been available to all of them. Now many exercises are accompanied by a reference to articles widely available online through university and college libraries (most are APA journals, in fact). In addition to such favorites as *Psychological Science* and *Developmental Psychology*, there are examples from journals whose existence might come as a surprise to many students, such as *Psychology, Public Policy, and Law*; *Psychological Trauma: Theory, Research, Practice, and Policy*; *Psychology of Aesthetics, Creativity, and the Arts*; and *Cultural Diversity and Ethnic Minority Psychology*.

Third, I have added some quick lists on the inside front and back covers. I hope these will be helpful for students as they begin to memorize rules they will need to use often.

In addition to these global changes, I have expanded sections on self-plagiarism, using "wiki" sources, referencing electronic sources, creating tables and graphs, and preparing posters.

Acknowledgments

Many people participated in the process of preparing this book. Most important are my students and colleagues at Barry University. Frequent discussions among the psychology faculty about our students' writing led me to try new ways of introducing this material to my experimental psychology classes. Through their comments and their progress, those students, in turn, provided feedback on my exercises. Using the fourth edition of this book with classes provided me with feedback about the ways it could be improved for the current edition.

I am grateful to colleagues who provided specific insights for the previous edition, and these sections are still present in the fifth edition. I thank Christopher Starratt for his conversations and advice about annotated bibliographies and Marjorie Loring for introducing me to some of the common wisdom about PowerPoint.

I want to thank Margaret Gatz for her encouragement and kind words at the Psychology of Aging Institute at the College of St. Scholastica in Duluth. She has been generous with guidance based on her vast experience as a journal editor.

The people at Cengage have been great collaborators. Jon-David Hague has been an excellent resource. He and Rebecca Rosenberg have been patient while we waited for the sixth edition of the *Publication Manual*. I'm grateful to Rebecca for shepherding the current edition. I also appreciate the fine work of Carrie Wagner and the rest of the production team at Pre-PressPMG.

I wish to thank the following reviewers who made helpful suggestions for this revision:

William Ashton, York College—City University of New York

Maria Bartini, Massachusetts College of Liberal Arts

Mike Hauser, Old Dominion University

Juliana K. Leding, University of North Florida

Paul C. LoCasto, Quinnipiac University

Their comments and suggestions were thoughtful and practical.

Finally, no professor-wife-mother manages to complete a successful manuscript without a lot of sacrifice from her husband and children. Paula and Jeff were still very present during the year that I worked on the proposal for the first edition of this book. Now, living with their own families and publishing as professional writers themselves, they continue to influence my thinking, and I appreciate their ongoing support for this project. In fact, Jeff, while still in college, canvassed journals with me while I was working on the first edition. He found some of the sentences that I used as examples in the exercises in this text and then tweaked them with his wry humor. And Mark, my husband, best friend, and closest colleague, reads manuscripts, patiently reads them again, and then arranges proper settings on computer programs because form and content both count.

Lenore T. Szuchman

About the Author

Asha Fuller

Lenore T. Szuchman is a developmental psychologist who received her Ph.D. from Florida International University in1990. In her position as professor in the Department of Psychology at Barry University, she currently teaches several writing-intensive courses, including Experimental Psychology and Advanced Experimental Psychology. She is the author and coauthor of articles on social cognition in older adults. She has also supervised a wide range of master's theses and senior projects that have been presented at professional and student conferences regionally and nationally.

Dr. Szuchman majored in comparative literature at Brandeis University, where she immersed herself in great novels and mastered MLA style. She has an M.A. in special education from the University of Texas at Austin. Her teaching experience is varied, from first-grade at the American School in Buenos Aires to language arts classes in secondary school for learning disabled students in Miami, Florida. Thus, she has had rich opportunities to shape her own and her students'writing abilities.

Students in Dr. Szuchman's Experimental Psychology classes conduct six experiments and write APA-style manuscripts focusing on all but the Introduction section. In Advanced Experimental Psychology, each student develops an independent research proposal and produces a complete Introduction and Method section, which often results in a senior thesis. Noticing the students' difficulties in making the transition from other types of college writing to the type required of scientific psychologists, Dr. Szuchman began to bring stacks of APA journals to class each week in her search for ways to train students to notice the differences between what they had been accustomed to reading and writing and what was now expected of them. Their valuable feedback in these classes shaped the final series of exercises produced for *Writing With Style.*

Writing With Style

CHAPTER 1

Introduction: The Laypeople and You

You have probably enjoyed reading books found on the psychology and self-help shelves of your local bookstore. Those books may have sparked your interest in psychology and made you think you might want to study psychology in college. The books were written to make psychology accessible to the general public. By now you should be thinking of those readers as laypeople. *You are no longer among them.* You are going to become a professional. You can and should read books written for laypeople, but you have to start writing like a psychologist.

You stopped being one of the laypeople when you finished your introductory psychology course and decided to major in psychology. You can now consider yourself a psychologist-in-training.

This book is designed to help you with the writing assignments you will face as a psychologist-in-training. The instructors who will grade your papers are accustomed to reading the articles of professional psychologists who publish in academic psychology journals. This type of writing differs from what you learned to do in English composition classes. And as strange as it might sound, it also differs from the writing in the books you may have been reading outside of class, the ones that got you interested in psychology in the first place—the books you found on the psychology shelves of your local bookstore. The best of those books translate the findings of scientific psychologists into language that makes them accessible and applicable for the nonscientific reader. But you are expected to write your research papers in an entirely different fashion because your training is in scientific psychology.

Scientific Psychology

Scientific psychology is not written in the same way as popular psychology. In contrast to pop psychology, scientific psychology meets the needs of the professional psychologist. This is a person who must keep up with new findings in a very broad literature. And because of the great amount of literature produced, the more similar the format is from article to article, the more accessible it is for this type of reader. For example, the Abstract section exists to help the reader make a quick decision about whether to read the article. By providing the same type of information about every article, the abstract facilitates decision making.

The professional reads different material with different levels of attention to detail. But not all professionals read with the same focus. The reader who is highly expert in a certain area of research might be interested in the Method section of an article above all. The psychologist who is reading at the outer edge of his or her expertise might read the Introduction section before deciding whether to finish the article. The person who skims needs to predict where the hypotheses will be and where the most important outcome will be. Finally, a student or researcher studying the area needs to see whether the reference list can point to further reading. You can see that if all parts of the article are written in a standardized way, each person's needs can be met efficiently. Sometimes this kind of writing does get repetitive for the sake of clarity, but it can still be interesting to read, and in the best examples, the prose is fluid and elegant. Certainly, one hopes that the research findings themselves generate excitement in at least a few readers. However, there can be no suspense, no teasing about the problem or its solution, no surprise endings. If generating suspense were important, the first thing to do would be to eliminate the abstract. Even topic sentences for paragraphs detract from suspense. If thrill were important, we would list results supporting the hypotheses first and losers last (rather than listing them in the sequence expected by the order of presentation of hypotheses). Surprise endings? Not for professionals; they may decide whether or not to read a research report only after knowing the ending (how the experiment came out).

Okay, you are ready to agree that professionals need a different prose style from the one intended for laypeople. But why do different professionals need different rules? Why can't everyone use MLA (Modern Language Association) or *Chicago Manual of Style* rules? One reason is that different professions rely on different methods and styles of argument. Scientists who do experiments need a different format from that of historians or literary critics. They have their own type of information to convey and their own values as consumers of their own literature. The American Psychological Association (APA) publishes many journals whose editors together consider thousands of submissions each year. The rules set forth in the *Publication Manual of the American Psychological Association,* sixth edition (2010), facilitate the handling of such a large number of manuscripts by standardizing much of the format. These rules have been so convenient for readers and writers that many other science and social science journals adhere to a similar framework. You might even be surprised to learn that the standards are available in Spanish, Portuguese, Korean, Chinese, and many other languages (p. xiv).

You will certainly want to own the *Publication Manual* or the *Concise Rules of APA Style* (American Psychological Association, 2010) and use one of them as a reference. But a reference book is just that—use it to look things up when you are not sure of a rule. You are not expected to memorize all of the rules. No psychologist submits a manuscript without consulting some rules in the *Publication Manual* along the way. Why bother to memorize the citation format for court decisions? for reviews of videos? for a non-English chapter in an edited book? What about the rule for brackets and parentheses? Do you use brackets within parentheses or parentheses within brackets? Look it up; we all do.

Many other conventions, however, require much greater attention because you will use them so often. Some of these are style rules you have encountered elsewhere, and it is time you mastered such rules as agreement of subject and verb, as well as when to use *between* versus *among.* Other conventions are unique to our field: Use past tense for the results and present tense for the conclusions; abbreviate more liberally in the abstract than in the body of the paper; and use metric units whenever possible.

Unfortunately, there is more to sounding like a psychologist than following all of those rules, just as there is more to sounding like a Texan than speaking English. If you want to sound like a Texan, you have to listen to many Texans talk. If you want to write like a psychologist, you have to read a great deal of psychology. But you have to begin to learn to write like a psychologist before you have the opportunity to read a lot of professional psychology. This book is designed to help get you there.

How to Use This Book

This is both a rule book and a workbook. It is designed to prepare you to write your first psychology research report or to help you improve your writing after you have had a bit of experience. It will guide you through the psychological literature in a way that will focus your attention on how authors use words and phrases. It will teach you to keep lists of examples of these words and phrases so that when you write papers, you can refer to your lists for models to help you construct sentences and paragraphs of your own. This book does *not* replace the *Publication Manual* or the *Concise Rules of APA Style.* When you write papers, you should keep one of those reference books and this filled-in workbook near you. This book is your sample book. If you want to produce a sentence or a phrase in a way that will let you pass as a more experienced writer of psychology papers than you are, use your lists. If you want to find out exactly how to organize, abbreviate, or punctuate a technical section, sentence, or phrase, use the *Publication Manual* or the *Concise Rules of APA Style.* By the way, when you use the *Publication Manual,* you might worry that it sometimes seems to contradict the printed format of the journals themselves. Your papers are known as *manuscripts,* and manuscripts differ from published material. Your responsibilities are those of the author of a manuscript, and you use rules based on the production of pages from your word processor.

You will find two types of exercises in this book. The first and most frequently presented will result in the lists of usable sentences and phrases just described. To produce these lists, use sentence frames; that is, leave blanks for the words that are specific to the research presented. For example, suppose you find the following sentence in a journal and it is an example of what you are looking for: "These findings regarding writing psychology papers have several implications." Copy it this way for your list of examples: "These findings regarding _____ have several implications." In most of the exercises, I have sampled several journals and filled in the first few items for you with frames from my own search. Sometimes I have filled in the blanks for fun. Feel free to do the same with your own examples.

The second type of exercise is designed to help you understand a point of grammar by finding examples of it. These are found exclusively in Chapter 10, "Grooming Tips for Psychology Papers." By doing the exercises, you should learn the rules and never have to look them up again.

Your instructor may guide you to the journals you should be looking at to do the various exercises. In all cases, APA journals will be suitable. However, you should be aware that, whereas most journals specialize in empirical research articles, others (notably, *Psychological Review* and *Psychological Bulletin*) publish theoretical and review articles. Unless otherwise noted, the assignments in this book require that you look at empirical research papers. Also, many important journals (e.g., *Child Development* and *Psychological Science*) are published by other organizations but adhere to APA guidelines. If your interest is primarily in one specific field of psychology, you can find out whether APA guidelines are followed by a non-APA journal in the section called Instructions to Authors printed in any current edition of that journal.

If your instructor has not specified which journals to use, my advice is to sample a variety of very recent sources. Go to your library's current periodicals area (or use your computer to locate some of these in your library's online journal collection) and find a single issue of five of the following journals:

Developmental Psychology

Health Psychology

International Journal of Stress Management

Journal of Applied Psychology

Journal of Comparative Psychology

Journal of Consulting and Clinical Psychology

Journal of Experimental Psychology: Applied

Journal of Experimental Psychology: Human Perception and Performance

Journal of Experimental Psychology: Learning, Memory, and Cognition

Journal of Family Psychology

Psychological Science

Psychology and Aging

Psychology of Religion and Spirituality

By sampling a range of topics, you are likely to find appropriate examples in at least one of them for any given exercise in this book.

If you look at online versions of journal articles rather than at hard copies, select PDF rather than HTML. The PDF format exactly reproduces the articles as they appear in print, so you can trust page numbers and the look of the graphics. The HTML version contains all of the words but not the visual form of the print version. Therefore, do not assume that formatting (such as italics) is preserved. For the same reason, you will have to consult hard copies of journals or PDF files when it is time to learn about tables and figures.

For many of the exercises, I have referred you to an article that contains an example that you can use. You may have access to this article through your college or university library. If you do not use that article to find the answer, there are many others available that will work. So feel free to use the one I noted or not. In any case, you will have to do some searching on your own to fill in all the blanks for the exercise.

Plagiarism

Students are often surprised to learn of the variety of behaviors that constitute *plagiarism.* In fact, much of the plagiarism found among college students is unintentional. But whether or not the behavior was intentional, the penalties can be severe. With plagiarism, as with criminal law, ignorance is no excuse. By working through this book, you have committed yourself to the effort of sharpening your writing skills. Therefore, it is also a good moment to consider the variety of misdeeds that you may accidentally commit when preparing your written work in scientific psychology.

Everyone seems to know that using someone else's words without giving that author credit is unacceptable. It does not matter whether you find these words in a journal article, in a friend's term paper, or on the Internet. This rule is quite simple to follow: Use quotation marks when you are using someone's exact words. Failing to do this is plagiarism whether or not you attribute the ideas to the proper person, because you have made it seem that the ideas may be borrowed but the words are your own.

A lot has been written lately about how easy plagiarism has become, now that students can cut and paste from the Internet. *The New York Times* (Rimer, 2003, September 3) reported on a study by Donald McCabe, a professor at Rutgers University, who found that 38% of undergraduate students said that in the last year they had done just that: cut and pasted from the Internet without citing the source. Nearly half of these students did not think that they had cheated. Perhaps this practice is made more appealing because much of what students find on the Internet does not seem to have an author or a date of publication. That does not mean, however, that stealing it is legal. It may mean that it has little intellectual value, and students should always be wary of using unsigned sources.

Often, students would like to paraphrase and give credit for the ideas, but they cannot think of original ways to express these ideas. Paraphrasing is a skill that takes some effort to acquire, so it is not surprising that when students find a useful thought in someone else's writing, they are stymied about how a paraphrase can ever be better than the original. Some turn to the thesaurus to solve the problem. They leave the sentence more or less the way it is but use a thesaurus to find words that might replace some of the words in the original author's sentence. With this type of "patchwork plagiarism," students assume that once they change some words, the sentence no longer requires quotation marks. Compounding this flawed strategy, they go on to think that if it does not need quotation marks, perhaps it does not even need to be credited to someone else at all. However, it is a secret little known to students that professors actually get some of their best laughs out of "thesaurus sentences."

Let me demonstrate. Here is the sentence at the end of the preceding paragraph after the thesaurus treatment: *It is a confidence obscure to scholars that gurus actually get their prime snorts out of thesaurus remarks.* Surely that is not what I meant to say. The fact that this does not convey the intended meaning is inconvenient, but the fact that it is still plagiarism may carry a severe penalty. In this example, the sentence *structure* has been plagiarized. You can't take someone else's sentence structure, replace a few words, and then call it your own. That's plagiarism.

There is a way to be fairly safe from unintentional plagiarism. Never try to paraphrase one sentence at a time. Instead, first read through the whole section you wish to paraphrase, and then write your paraphrase, but without looking at the original. Then, be sure to credit the *ideas* conveyed in the paraphrased sections to their author. If you must quote a phrase or a sentence, do so. But don't change the original just a bit and then think it is a paraphrase. When using Internet sources, print the whole document or take notes from the screen. Don't cut and paste for later paraphrase—treat the source just as you would an article photocopied at the library. A good guideline is to "use a little and give credit" (Talab, 2000, p. 7). In fact, that is just about the same advice

I could give for print sources. Once you have used a little from a number of sources, you have transformed the material into something of your own, and you have broken no laws.

Now that you have learned to avoid stealing someone's sentence structure, what about the structure of a larger unit? Suppose you find a literature review on the same subject as your own. What is the plagiarism risk in this case? If you organize the material around the same themes as someone else has done, you have plagiarized. If you use the same examples to make the same point, you have plagiarized. To prevent these forms of plagiarism, consider using the reference list of a literature review to help you with your own library work, but don't read the actual review article until you have drawn some conclusions of your own. Then, when you find that the review author has made a point you would like to add to your own review, you can cite that author for having had a certain insight about some research that you have also read—but that did not provide you with the same insight. You can even cite the author of the literature review for finding themes in the literature that organized the topic in a useful way.

What about borrowing ideas from your professor or your textbook? To be safe, you must give credit in those cases as well. You may be expected to get your knowledge from these sources, but if you use that knowledge in a written product of your own, cite the sources.

Although students don't usually define it as plagiarism, it is also unethical to use your own words more than once as if you had written them fresh each time. This is called self-plagiarism. "Just as researchers do not present the work of others as their own (plagiarism), they do not present their own previously published work as new scholarship (self-plagiarism)" (APA, 2010, p. 16). Each professor expects that work written to fulfill the requirements of a certain class be submitted only for that class. And no one is allowed to sell a product as new if it has already been used. If you have a paper already written that seems to serve the needs of another assignment, check with the second professor for guidance about how much of the paper needs to be refreshed before you recycle it for the second class. APA guidelines suggest that the "core" of the work should be original each time, but that it may be necessary to repeat some material that has previously been published in order to develop the new argument or amplify it. However, researchers are expected to cite their own previous work when they refer to it.

Students sometimes have trouble deciding when a statement needs a reference and when it does not. You do not need to cite someone else for your own opinions or for generally agreed-upon facts or principles. Your own opinion is easy to identify. By contrast, it may be difficult to decide which facts are generally agreed upon. It is tempting to assume that everyone sees behavior exactly as you do. For example, most observers may agree that adolescence is a time when self-esteem is fragile. But wait. Are you as sure about that as you are about the fact that in the United States, adolescents are expected to attend school? In fact, when you talk about psychological constructs such as self-esteem, you are very near the divide between fact and nonfact. If you cannot find a reference for your assertion about self-esteem, at least hedge it a bit. Perhaps you can assert that there *seems* to be an emphasis in our culture on the fragility of adolescent self-esteem. If you have really searched the literature on self-esteem, then you will have references at your disposal to cite when you make an assertion. Cite them, and you are safe.

Students who are new to a field may also be confused about when a phrase is a standard technical term and when it is an original term. You are free to use technical phrases without attribution. Usually, it is safe to use effects that authors study (e.g., transfer of training) or variables they use (e.g., test anxiety) without quotation marks. If you use a short phrase that you are not sure should be attributed to an author, use no quotation marks, but do include a page reference (as you would in a direct quote) along with the rest of the citation information.

You may have begun to wonder how you can be safe from plagiarism if you are copying sentences from published sources into this book for later use in your own papers. The reason you can do that is the same reason you can use a dictionary or a book of foreign phrases without fear of plagiarism. You need to learn how words are used before you can use them on your own. People who share a subculture, as do scholars in any discipline, tend to use words and even whole phrases in a particular way. As you do the exercises in this book, you will find that the same phrases keep appearing in the articles you scan. You may even have difficulty finding enough different examples of a given type to fill the spaces provided. As rich as the English language is, only a finite number of ways exist for phrasing a prediction or the results of a *t* test. When a form is used repeatedly, you are allowed to use it without fear that someone else "owns" it.

A lot of the discussion about plagiarism, here and in other parts of your educational experience, is presented as a series of rules you have to follow to avoid getting into trouble. It is important to take a moment to consider the main reason that scholars do not plagiarize. There is tremendous satisfaction in doing good research, writing good manuscripts, having original ideas, and explaining them coherently, even elegantly if possible. That satisfaction is not to be had when some part of the material or some of the ideas are stolen from someone else or when data are fabricated. Scholars in an academic field usually love their jobs and put in far more hours than would be required in most other professions. They do this because it brings them joy. My observation is that students also get great pleasure from a job well done, and that kind of pleasure does not come from claiming someone else's accomplishments as one's own.

My Style in This Book Should Not Be Your Style for a Research Report

In preparing this book, I have considered my own role as a model for your writing. I have explained that technical writing is formal. A formal tone does not, for example, speak to the reader as "you." The articles you will read are designed to inform, not to amuse. Journal articles do not contain informal language, slang, contractions, or humor. If I were to write this book in that tone, it would be a good example for you, but it would not serve my purpose. Undoubtedly, you already write differently for different purposes. Now that you are learning the rules of a scientific style for a new purpose, I do not recommend that you model your scientific prose from novels, newspapers, or textbooks—or any sources other than those specifically written in APA style. Textbooks do not necessarily benefit from such a style. Therefore, I have chosen not to conform strictly to APA style in this book. However, I hope that you will not catch me making spelling, grammar, or punctuation errors.

CHAPTER *2*

Some Generalizations About How Psychologists Write

Referring to Other Authors

One of the most common topics that psychologists and psychology students write about is each other. In fact, the longest part of a published research study is usually the introduction, in which the author surveys the research that led to the current study. Advanced students and researchers often write research proposals that emphasize the same type of material found in the introductions of printed articles. Finally, undergraduate and graduate students are often assigned to write literature reviews as term papers. Therefore, it is very important to learn what the *Publication Manual* has to say about conveying the ideas and findings of other authors. Similarly, it is valuable to search some journals to see what generalizations can be made about the unwritten rules.

When you refer to the work of another author or authors, use last names only, and do not mention the titles of their works. The publication year is a necessary part of the citation, but it is seldom presented as part of the sentence. Students often write, "In 2010, Smith did a study of . . ." However, it is much more appropriate to keep the year in parentheses unless you are making a special point of the date. When referring to the same study twice within a single paragraph, do not include the year after the first instance, unless there is the possibility of confusing the reader about two studies by the same author published in different years.

▲ **REMINDER BOX** ▼

Refer to other authors by last name only and do not mention the titles of their works (except in the References section).

You have the option of inserting the author's name and year of publication in parentheses: "A study of X has revealed dramatic changes over the last decade (Smith, 2010)." If you do this, however, you must not also include the author in the body of the same sentence. An example of this type of error is the following sentence: "Smith's study of X has revealed dramatic changes over the last decade (Smith, 2010)." Your best bet would be to keep the author and the year in parentheses. Normally, the point of your sentence is what the author did, not who the author is. On those rare occasions when you do wish to name a theorist or compare the work of two authors, then you can pull the name out of the parentheses and put it in the sentence.

Another problem with regard to citations is how to refer to works that you have not read. First, try to get every relevant article and read it. However, instructors understand that undergraduate students are more likely than published authors to cite materials from secondary sources. Be aware that this does not allow you to put the sources you have not read yourself (primary original sources) in your reference list. Put the source you *read* in the References section. In the body of the paper, you can mention the original work and indicate that you found mention of it in a secondary source, which you *do* cite. Example: "Skinner (as cited in Garfield, 2000) found no evidence of emotion in rats." Garfield will be on your reference list; Skinner will not. It is probably wise to assume that you will need to cite exclusively primary sources after your undergraduate work—for your master's thesis and everything that follows.

▲ **REMINDER BOX** ▼

If you have not read a source, do not list it in your References section. In the body of the paper, refer to the source you did read (secondary source) and indicate that the primary source was cited in the secondary source.

A potential source of confusion exists when someone else's research is referred to as the "current" study, the "present" study, or "this" study. These terms always refer to the study being reported in the Method and Results sections of the article you are reading (or the research report you are writing). When you are looking at an article and writing about the outcome of that author's study in your own paper, you may come across one of these phrases, and it may find its way into your description of that study. Do not do this. You may confuse your readers even more than this paragraph has confused you! And for the same reason.

▲ REMINDER BOX ▼

Do not use "the current study" or "the present study" to refer to someone else's work.

Psychologists are very polite when disagreeing with or disapproving of colleagues. You should be sensitive to this tone in your own reviews of the literature. A psychologist who feels that Smith has done a terrible study may only say, "Other researchers have failed to replicate Smith's result" or "Smith may have failed to take into account the . . ." Also be careful about your tone when describing a controversial issue. Present both sides and indicate what kind of data support one conclusion and what kind support the other.

Words and Phrases to Collect

The English language contains so many words and expressions that it may come as a surprise to learn how often psychologists use the same ones over and over again. This is actually of benefit to the new writer because with a collection of stock words and phrases, anyone can *sound* like a psychologist even while still learning to *think* like one. In this section you will create a collection of some of these words and phrases to sprinkle in your own writing.

First, consider how often sentences in a literature review are constructed around a researcher or a research study as the grammatical subject. For example, "Garfield (2001) demonstrated that . . ." You may be tempted to vary your sentences, choosing the author sometimes, the research study at other times. Be cautious about this. You are obligated to use verbs that logically suit the abilities of your grammatical subjects. People are capable of many activities (verbs), but experiments can hardly do anything. Consider this problem whenever you are tempted to begin a sentence with "The study . . ." Exactly what can a study do?

> *At least one example for every exercise in this chapter can be found in this article:* Judge, T. A., Hurst, C., & Simon, L.S. (2009). Does it pay to be smart, attractive, or confident (or all three)? Relationships among general mental ability, physical attractiveness, core self-evaluations, and income. *Journal of Applied Psychology, 94,* 742–755.

You should find articles on your own to fill in the remaining blanks.

Exercise 1

Select several articles that cover topics of interest to you or that have been assigned in your course. Find verbs in which the grammatical subject of a sentence is someone's *study, work, experiment,* or *research.* It may also be useful to include the object of that verb.

1. employs methods

2. demonstrates

3. provides evidence

4. _____

5. _____

6. _____

Another nonhuman grammatical subject often found in research reports is the outcome of someone's research. The words to look for here are *findings, results,* and *evidence.* Do not be surprised if the list you create for this exercise has a lot of overlap with the previous one.

Exercise 2

List the verbs in sentences in which the subject is some kind of experimental *outcome.*

1. demonstrates

2. can be explained

3. suggests

4. _____

5. _____

6. _____

What can theories do? What can be done to them?

Exercise 3

Find the verbs or verb phrases that are used with *theories* or *hypotheses*.

1. take something as evidence

2. have been challenged

3. focus on

4. lead to the hypothesis that

5. _____

6. _____

7. _____

You may have noticed in completing the previous three exercises that authors often use passive verb constructions when discussing a study, an outcome, or a theory. For example, they will note that a study *was designed* for some purpose. That type of writing shows you that the author knows that studies themselves cannot assess or find or test. Authors design studies so that they (the authors) can assess things. In contrast to inanimate studies and abstractions such as theories, a researcher or group of researchers can very easily be the grammatical subject of a sentence. In this case, look for sentences in which the subject is a specific author or authors or a more general noun such as *author, researcher,* or *experimenter.*

Exercise 4

List the verbs associated with *researchers.* (Here, you have been given plenty of space for a long list.) When you find a word more than once, put a check mark next to it every time you find it.

1. have shown
2. found
3. replicated
4. reported

5. _____

6. _____

7. _____

8. _____

9. _____

10. _____

11. _____

12. _____

13. _____

14. _____

15. _____

▲ REMINDER BOX ▼

Use a person (e.g., "the researcher" or a proper name) rather than a product (e.g., study, experiment, or finding) as a sentence subject whenever possible.

Now that you know 15 terms that psychologists *do* use, please take note of the words you did *not* find. You probably did not find *feel*. Research studies cannot feel, and researchers keep their feelings to themselves. Also, you probably found less *thinking* and *believing* than you might have expected. Perhaps *believe* doesn't convey the scientific attitude as well as the word *hypothesize* does. Likewise, researchers very often *reason*, but it seems as if they hardly ever *think*. Another type of word that will be rare on your lists is related to writing and talking: *stated, wrote, said*. Journalists report what people say and write. Psychologists use the writings of others to report what they found or investigated.

▲ **REMINDER BOX** ▼

Do not indicate what researchers thought, felt, believed, or said.

Another type of verb that psychologists use can be categorized as a "hedge word." We hedge even when we hold strong opinions about why people behave as they do, because usually we cannot be absolutely sure of cause and effect. Even the most carefully designed experiments do not provide ironclad evidence so that we can generalize with absolute certainty about behavior. Therefore, we avoid using confident language (e.g., the kind you just read in the previous sentence) when we are making claims about behavior. *May* and *might* are our primary hedge words: certain functions *may* decline with age; it *may* be fruitful to consider *x* in the context of *y*. Sometimes we hedge outside of the verb phrase; for example, "One possible interpretation is . . ." Also, don't forget that hypothesis testing is another excuse for a hedge word.

For example, results *support* a hypothesis; they seldom *confirm* it; and they NEVER *prove* it.

Exercise 5

List some hedge words from your articles.

1. suggests

2. appears to

3. is consistent with

4. _____

5. _____

6. _____

Transition words and phrases help to connect the discussion of one study with that of another. They also guide the reader through the logic of the sequence of paragraphs. They can make your writing more precise. Look for them at the beginning of paragraphs, set off by commas.

Exercise 6

List transition words and phrases. These are often at the beginning of paragraphs, but other words can hold that place as well. When you find a word or phrase at the beginning of a paragraph set off by a comma from the rest of the sentence, ask yourself whether it helps to connect that sentence to the previous paragraph. If it does, put it on this list.

1. Notably,

2. In contrast,

3. Similarly,

4. _____

5. _____

6. _____

7. _____

8. _____

A common mistake is using a transition by itself (such as *on the other hand*) that requires the explicit use of a preceding one (*on one hand*). Also, if you are going to enumerate your points, use *first, second,* and *third*—not *firstly, secondly*, and *thirdly*. And don't use *second* if you have not been explicit about *first*.

Words and Phrases to Avoid

The *Publication Manual* offers many examples of writing errors to avoid. This section merely highlights some common student bloopers. It would be wise for you also to look over the chapter entitled "Writing Clearly and Concisely" in the *Publication Manual* or "Concise and Bias-Free Writing" in the *Concise Rules*.

First, Don't Forget the "No-No's" We Have Already Covered

1. Don't use the *current* or *present* study when referring to someone else's work in your literature review.

2. Don't mention authors' first names.

3. Don't provide the titles of articles you discuss in your literature review. They belong only in the References section.

4. Don't use the word *prove*. (Substitute the word *support*.)

5. Don't fool yourself into thinking that you know the feelings and thoughts of the researchers you cite.

6. Don't refer to what other authors *stated, said,* or *wrote.*

Wordiness and Redundancy

Wordiness and redundancy are not the same. You should avoid using more words than you need (for example, *based on the fact that* is not as efficient as *because*), and you should also try not to say the same thing twice (e.g., *could be perhaps because* is not as good as *could be because*). Your main concern, however, is to eliminate all unnecessary words. Do not bother doing this until you have completed the drafts related to organization and clarity. But by the time you are on your third or fourth draft (I realize that I am asking you to commit yourself to quite a few drafts!), look for words that you can cross out without changing any meanings. Here are examples:

1. *The results revealed that* . . . Omit the entire phrase and start your sentence with the word that would come next.

2. *The obtained data showed* . . . Where else would data come from if it had not been obtained by someone? Just say *the data showed* . . .

3. *Participants for the study were* . . . Of course they were for the study. Just say *Participants were* . . .

4. *Due to the fact that* . . . Just say *because* . . .

5. *The reason is because* . . . Just say *the reason is* . . . The same goes for *the reasons behind why* . . .

6. *A total of eight participants* . . . Just say *eight participants* . . .

7. *The results were statistically significant.* This is science you are reporting. Of course you are using *significant* in its statistical sense. Omit *statistically*.

8. . . . *has been previously found.* Past tense verb, so it must have occurred previously. Omit *previously*.

9. *In his study, Smith found* . . . Of course that's where he found it. Omit *in his study*.

10. *Distinctly different* . . . Choose one.

11. *Memory recall* . . . Choose one.

Overreliance on Passive Voice

The *Publication Manual* advises us to "prefer the active voice" (p. 77). That seems to allow some flexibility—especially when you want to emphasize what was done rather than who did it. But sometimes writers get so tangled up in sentences that they don't realize how easy changing to the active voice can be. Here are some common examples:

1. *Participants were administered a questionnaire (drug, test, interview, and so on).* Examiners can administer tests. But as a result, *tests* are administered, not participants. What do participants do? *They take a test. They fill in* or *complete* a questionnaire.

2. *The experiment was designed by Smith to* . . . This type of construction is easy to turn into the active voice: *Smith designed an experiment to* . . .

Informal Language and Slang

The tone of technical writing is not colloquial—that is, it is not conversational or informal. The *Publication Manual* provides the example of *write up*, which is an informal, perhaps imprecise, way of saying *report*. Slang is the most informal type of language. Examples include the use of *blooper* to mean *error* and *no-no* to mean *something that is forbidden*. (Notice that my use of these words is legal—I am not writing a research report.) Students usually know that slang is a *no-no*, and they avoid that type of *blooper*. But you must be on the lookout (that is, *search*) for informal language in your technical writing.

1. *Contractions are absolutely forbidden.* Use apostrophes only to indicate possession. Remember that when pronouns contain possessive meanings, they do so without apostrophes *(e.g., its, hers)*.

2. Do not be afraid to use *because*. *Because* is a lovely, precise word. *Being that is* a poor replacement. *Since* is specifically made illegal for this purpose in the *Publication Manual*. *Since* is used to mean *after that time*.

3. Use *while* (like *since*) in its temporal sense only. Hunt for *while* in your papers. If you cannot substitute *simultaneously*, perhaps you should consider *although, and,* or *whereas*.

4. Do not be afraid to use *and.* Indulge yourself. *And* is often the best substitute for *while.* See how many wordy phrases you can kill by replacing them with *and.*

Long Quotations and Frequent Short Quotations

Because we strive for clarity and economy of expression, there is seldom need for a long quotation. Literary criticism, by contrast, would be nowhere without the long quotation. The way someone else says something is vital to what literary critics have to say about it. But technical styles are seldom quotable. If you are reporting on someone else's research, just summarize the author's point. Perhaps the author has used a word in a new way; if so, place quotation marks around that word. There are rules about how to cite page numbers when quoting from another's work (in parentheses after the close quotation mark) and special rules about indenting long quotations. You should use the indented form only for long passages (40 or more words), for example, when you are quoting from your own experimental materials or instructions to participants. See Chapter 8 in this book for more information on quotation format.

It is easy to sympathize with someone who would like to avoid plagiarism and avoid short quotations at the same time. Sometimes you might feel that there is no efficient way to convey the contents of a certain phrase (e.g., "responses were scored for speed and accuracy") except in the author's words. One way to solve this is to take a stretch and get a drink of water when you feel a short quotation coming on. Then when you sit down to write again, write that sentence without looking at the source. If it still comes out very close to the original, you can put the page reference in at the end of the paraphrase.

▲ REMINDER BOX ▼
Avoid long quotations and frequent brief quotations.

The Editorial We

Students are often taught (in classes other than psychology) that the use of *I* is to be avoided and that one alternative is to refer to yourself in the third person: the author. In psychology papers, however, that is absolutely out of the question. What remains is to refer to yourself as *we.*

This is called the "editorial we" (as distinct from the "royal we," which kings and queens use to refer to themselves). It is common in some styles to use the editorial we, but the *Publication Manual* expressly advises against it.

You are allowed to use *we* to refer to yourself as author, however, if your paper has more than one author. Also, you are perfectly within your rights to use *I* in a psychology paper. If that bothers you, feel free to design the sentence some other way. Sometimes the passive voice can be used instead, though usually with less than optimal results: "It was hypothesized that . . . ."

The best solution is to take yourself right out of the sentence: "The hypothesis was . . . ." In general, you should try to place yourself in the background of the narrative. After all, it is not about you. The emphasis should be on your ideas, your findings, the participants, and so on. When you discuss other authors, this point of view comes naturally. When you discuss what *you* did, it becomes more difficult. You will find more suggestions about how to focus away from yourself in Chapter 4 on the Method section.

▲ REMINDER BOX ▼

Do not refer to yourself as "we."

The Use of "You"

Do not affect a tone that implies an interaction with the reader. In a research report, there is never a reason to refer to the reader of the work (as I have done throughout this textbook). Neither is it permitted to use the word *you* instead of *one* in speaking of a hypothetical person. For example, "When you reach middle age, your vision and hearing have already begun to decline." This should be written in the third person: "When one reaches middle age, one's vision and hearing have already begun to decline." Very often, sentences containing *you* should be rewritten without reference to anyone: "By middle age, vision and hearing have already begun to decline." *People* is a word that can come in handy too: "When people reach middle age, their vision and hearing have already begun to decline."

▲ REMINDER BOX ▼

Do not call the reader "you."

The One-Sentence Paragraph

This is a rule you learned many years ago and should not give up now. The style you are trying to achieve is crisp, clear, and well organized. Therefore, it is likely that putting a topic sentence at the beginning of every paragraph will enhance the effect. Putting such a sentence elsewhere in the paragraph (as you may have been encouraged to do previously for the sake of variety) detracts from the goal. If you find that you have written a one-sentence paragraph, you must evaluate the organizational plan that allowed that to happen. What is the topic of this paragraph? Is this sentence a topic sentence that would benefit from further elaboration? If so, perhaps you forgot to elaborate. Is your single sentence really a bit of elaboration that belongs elsewhere (for example, tied to a topic that already has its own paragraph)? If so, then move it. Is it by itself because it is actually all you really know about that subject? Perhaps your paper would be improved if you omitted material you know so little about.

▲ REMINDER BOX ▼

Start every paragraph with a topic sentence and never write one-sentence paragraphs.

Overstatement

It is very tempting to fall into the habit of overstatement. When you write that "it is absolutely essential" that a certain type of study be done, that is an exaggeration, isn't it? You are probably not looking at an "enormous" problem in our society either. Nor is a scientific report the place to discuss the "tragedy" of AIDS. On some level, all of those statements might be correct, but they are not found in professional journals.

Sexist Language

You probably know that it is no longer acceptable to use *he* when you are referring to a person who might be male or female. The *Publication Manual* advises that you not use the unpronounceable combination form *s/he* or *(s)he*. It is also not acceptable to alternate *he* and *she* as if either form could be used generically. You may use *he or she*, but sentences become unnecessarily cumbersome when you do: "The participant filled out his or her questionnaire using his or her code number." Of the various alternatives, try to find one that eliminates the need for the singular pronoun completely. Using *his or her* every time you find that you need a possessive is not as convenient as using *their*. However, be sure that you have used a plural noun prior to replacing it with a plural pronoun. It is a common error to begin the sentence with an individual and then talk about *their score*. If you begin with one person, you must then refer to *his or her score*. One solution is to begin with the plural (people, participants, students, etc.) and then discuss *their scores*. You have thereby avoided both gender bias and an inappropriate pronoun. For the preceding example, a solution would be "Participants filled out their questionnaires using their code numbers." Another solution would be use an article (the, a) instead of a pronoun: "Each participant filled out the questionnaire using a code number.

▲ REMINDER BOX ▼

Do not write *he* when you mean *he or she*. Do your best to avoid the situation at all.

Using Prefixes as If They Were Words

A few prefixes are used quite often in psychology papers. They include *non, pre, post*, and *sub*. Please remember that prefixes cannot stand alone with spaces on both sides. They must be attached to words. They may be attached with hyphens or just stuck onto the root words; the *Publication Manual* will guide you if you are not sure in a given case. (See Table 4.2 in the *Publication Manual* or Table 2.2 in the *Concise Rules*.) But you can be very sure that if they stand alone, you have made a mistake. If you tested nonsmokers and smokers in your experiment, be sure that you have not written *non smokers* instead of *nonsmokers*.

A general rule in APA style is that most prefixes do not take hyphens. Sometimes that makes words seem odd (like *posttest*), so be prepared. The only prefix we use frequently that *does* take a hyphen is *self*. So enjoy having self-esteem, doing self-scoring, and being self-conscious. And get used to subtest scores, counterbalanced groups, interracial dyads, and intertrial intervals.

There are also some extra reasons for hyphens with prefixes. Ones you might need are the following: if the base word is capitalized (*mini-Pavlovian*), if it is a number (*pre-1957*), or if it is an abbreviation (*non-PTSD group*).

▲ REMINDER BOX ▼

Do not leave prefixes hanging by themselves.

Incorrect Plurals

Many professors will be annoyed if you do not use the following plurals correctly: *data, criteria, phenomena, stimuli,* and *hypotheses.* The singular forms are *datum, criterion, phenomenon, stimulus,* and *hypothesis.* You will probably never need to use *datum,* but try learning the other four right now. And please remember to use the plural verb form when you use plural nouns (e.g., data *were* gathered, the hypotheses *were* supported).

▲ REMINDER BOX ▼

These words are plural nouns: data, criteria, phenomena, stimuli, and hypotheses.

Mixed-Up Latin Abbreviations

You probably find yourself writing *et al., i.e.,* and *e.g.* a lot now. But where do the periods and commas really go? The commas go after *i.e.* and *e.g.* every time you write them. What about the periods? The periods go after abbreviations. Here is what these three abbreviations mean:

1. *Et al.* stands for *et alia,* which means "and other things." If you remember that *et* is not an abbreviation but rather a Latin word meaning "and," then you will remember that there is no reason to put a period after it. By contrast, *al.* is an abbreviation, so it requires a period.

2. *I.e.* stands for *id est,* the Latin phrase meaning "that is." Both letters in this Latin abbreviation are legitimate abbreviations, so they both take periods. If you need this phrase, use the Latin abbreviation inside parentheses and the English phrase "that is" outside parentheses. Either way, they are followed by a comma.

3. *E.g.* stands for *exempli gratia,* the Latin phrase meaning "for example." As with *i.e.,* these letters are both abbreviations, so both take

periods. Also, as above, if you use the phrase inside parentheses, use the Latin abbreviation, and use the English equivalent outside the parentheses. Either way, follow it with a comma.

Don't use italics with these abbreviations in your own writing.

▲ **REMINDER BOX** ▼

Learn how to punctuate *i.e., e.g.,* and *et al.*

Looking Back and Looking Ahead

In this Chapter, I have called your attention to some unexpected APA style quirks and some professorial pet peeves. In addition to my own experience with students, I have selected topics based on ideas from my colleagues, some anonymous reviewers, my students, and my own leapfrogging through the *Publication Manual.*

You have learned some conventions about referring to other authors: to refer to them by their last names, to be polite about their shortcomings, and to be mindful of the differences between primary and secondary sources. You have learned to be precise in your word choices: verbs that suit your sentence subjects; words that avoid ascribing feelings to other psychologists when their reasoning is what we care about; hedge words rather than overconfident ones; transition words; unbiased language. I have urged you to avoid wordiness and redundancy, informal language, and overuse of quotations. Do not call yourself "we" and do not call the reader "you." Be conscious of tight organization of paragraphs, always using topic sentences at the start. Spelling has become a little more complicated for you. You have new hyphen rules to learn as well as some special plural forms. And you even managed to learn a little Latin!

The next chapter will involve less leapfrogging. The parts of the research report begin to come into focus with an in-depth look at the introduction. You will see that a good bit of what you have to learn is quite standardized, and once learned, the format can be used for many of your papers.

For more information:

Topic	Publication Manual	Concise Rules
Referring to the same study twice in one paragraph	6.11	7.12
Secondary sources	6.17	7.18
Tone	3.07	1.07
Fairness	2.05	—
Think, feel	3.09	1.09
Transition words	3.05, 3.21	1.05, 1.21
Wordiness Redundancy	3.08	1.08
Passive voice	3.18	1.18
Informal language	3.09	1.09
Since/because/while	3.22	1.22
Quotations	4.07, 6.03	2.08, 7.03
He or she	3.12	1.12
We	3.09	1.09
Prefixes/hyphens	4.13	2.14
Incorrect plurals	4.12	2.13
Latin abbreviations	4.26	3.07

CHAPTER 3

Preparing the Introduction Section and the Literature Review Paper

The introduction should answer the following questions about the research you have done:

1. Why should a reader care? Why is this important? Is it important enough to merit (more) research? By the way, is there some controversy about this? Is it a social problem to be solved perhaps? What, exactly, is the purpose?

2. Assuming that the reader knows something about all this without exactly being a specialist, what research and theory does that reader need to know about in order to see where this new work fits in?

3. What are the hypotheses and what are their rationales? And which are the main ones and which are secondary? How does the research design employed here have the potential to test these hypotheses and serve that original purpose?

4. What are the theoretical and practical implications?

You will find that authors are often explicit about these items. An article may even begin with the words "The purpose of the study was . . ." The final paragraphs of the introduction may contain sentences that begin with "The specific hypotheses were . . ." In between, you will find the literature review and theoretical implications of the current study.

Begin your introduction on a new page. Type the title of your paper centered at the top, and capitalize important words. Do not use the word *Introduction* as a heading for this section. Its location indicates what section it is. In the publications themselves, however, sometimes the word *Introduction* does appear as a heading. Remember that the *Publication Manual* is directing authors of manuscripts, not printers of journals.

▲ REMINDER BOX ▼
The Introduction section does not include the label "Introduction."

What Was Done and Why

If you look a little more closely, you find that the *Publication Manual* advises that the first paragraph or two should provide "a firm sense of what was done and why" (p. 27).

Exercise 1

Select several articles from a variety of journals or use articles that have been assigned by your professor. Examining only the first two paragraphs of your research articles, copy the single sentence in each that states the purpose of the study. If you do not find such a sentence, try the last two paragraphs of the introduction.

1. Accordingly, the primary purpose of our study is to reexamine the findings of Lector (1999), taking into consideration the number of hours of food deprivation.

2. This research was conducted to determine variables that characterize beach umbrella dealers who show escalation in rude behavior during the winter months.

3. Elephants are always larger than turtles. In the present study, we attempted to find a possible explanation for this striking finding.

4. _____

   _____

5. _____

_____

6. _____

_____

Exercise 2

Still looking only at the first or last few paragraphs, find and copy sentences that indicate why this is an important research issue.

1. Knowledge of these factors may help identify individuals at risk for . . .

2. The problem under study here has been implicated in many psychological theories as vitally important to the functioning of . . .

3. As knowledge of the consequences of x has increased, investigators have become interested in . . .

4. _____

_____

5. _____

_____

6. _____

_____

Now consider how authors introduce their work. The first sentence of an article is always written with some strategy in mind. The author might want to demonstrate the importance of the issue or the purpose at the start. Or there might be other attention-grabbing ways to begin. But this is the place to beware of the temptation to overstate, as was noted in Chapter 2. Assume that the reader is trained in the general area of psychology you are writing about. For example, you do not need to note that health psychologists have long researched unhealthy behaviors and so it is important to study smoking cessation. They also know that lots and lots of people smoke, so it is not necessary to attempt the journalistic technique of telling the reader just how many there are. It would be more appropriate to note that despite great efforts at research about smoking and the implementation of smoking cessation programs, some percentage of people continue to smoke. That is the sort of fact that would tempt a psychologist to read on.

Exercise 3

Copy the first sentence from several articles. Indicate what type of information it contains. It is possible that some of the sentences you found for the previous two exercises held this place of honor in an article. For this exercise, however, do not recycle specific sentences from the previous exercises.

1. A growing body of literature indicates that interactions with their owners can have a critical impact on the well-being of pets. (A statement of a long-studied problem.)

2. Given the paucity of information on [my topic] and the strong impact it has on [something the reader is concerned about], this study examined [something that has not been studied, but should be].

3. Fear of death can be defined as . . . (A definition.)

4. Elderly male residents of assisted living facilities who still maintain their ability to drive at night are very popular indeed. (A statement of a well-known phenomenon.)

5. Persons over the age of 110 often flood counseling centers with their marital problems. (Alarming but little-known statistics.)

6. _____

   _____

7. _____

   _____

8. _____

   _____

Exercise 4

Now look at the final few paragraphs of the introduction. Find the specific hypotheses. Copy the phrases that indicate that these are *hypotheses*.

Look for such words as *predict* or *expect* if you do not see what you are looking for right away.

1. Specific predictions were as follows . . .

2. Experience with vegetables should affect the way in which babies understand differences between peas and carrots.

3. The use of hot peppers was expected to enhance the flavor of the pizza.

4. _____

_____

5. _____

_____

6. _____

_____

Hypotheses need rationales—they are not supposed to be based on intuition or hunches. It is possible that early on in the research process an experimenter did have a hunch. That hunch may even have led the researcher to begin the project, perhaps by beginning a literature search to support that hunch. By the time the literature has been reviewed, the author is supposed to be able to support the hypotheses with something more convincing than his or her original hunch. Researchers normally use previous results or theories to predict how they expect an experiment to come out. When writing your hypothesis, you are expected to provide the reasons why, for example, one group will score higher than another or why one manipulation will yield overestimations and another will yield underestimations of a measured weight. This process is implicit in the entire literature review contained in the introduction. But it is good practice to make these reasons explicit at the point where the hypotheses are discussed.

Exercise 5

Find examples of explicit rationales for hypotheses.

1. If there are qualitative differences between the common cold and the Ebola virus, differences in their effects on behavior could be expected.

2. From prior research with various primate groups, cognitively based grooming strategies were expected to be evident in humans.

3. Because our prior analysis pointed to the importance of avoiding alcohol when driving . . .

   This article has 3 (or use other articles of your choice): Salomon, K., Clift, A., Karlsdóttir, M., & Rottenberg, J. (2009). Major depressive disorder is associated with attenuated cardiovascular reactivity and impaired recovery among those free of cardiovascular disease. *Health Psychology, 28*, 157–165.

4. _____

   _____

5. _____

   _____

6. _____

   _____

Note that hypotheses often state a direction. That is, they make predictions that one group will perform better than another, not just differently. In example 3 above, it might be expected specifically that the alcohol-impaired drivers would not drive as well as the unimpaired group—not simply that one group (unspecified) would not drive as well as the other. When hypotheses do not contain a predicted direction of effect, they are sometimes called *research questions*. For example, a researcher might wish to compare two types of support groups without a firm belief that one is better than the other. Sometimes these studies are called *descriptive*. In such cases, researchers want to learn *how* groups differ before they attempt to explain the reason or the mechanism for the difference. Another type of study may be designed so that one outcome would support one hypothesis and a different outcome would support a competing hypothesis. The research question would be posed in terms indicating which one of the two theories explaining a given phenomenon is more likely to be correct.

Exercise 6

Find examples of research questions. These are likely to be signaled by such words as *describe, explore,* and *assess.*

1. The present study investigated relations between Measure A and Measure B, indexing two dimensions of . . .

2. We asked whether [this] and [that] explain differences between two groups of individuals.

3. The present study is designed to assess the role of love relationships in the life of one-celled organisms. Lack of such data represents an important gap in the literature.

   This article contains 3 research questions (or use other articles of your choice): Lippke, S., Ziegelmann, J. P., Schwarzer, R., & Velicer, W. F. (2009). Validity of stage assessment in the adoption and maintenance of physical activity and fruit and vegetable consumption. *Health Psychology, 28*, 183–193.

4. _____

   _____

5. _____

   _____

6. _____

   _____

In trying to provide "a firm sense of what was done and why," writers sometimes have difficulty deciding how much methodological detail is appropriate in the introduction. You should find statements referring to the method of the study being reported. Authors use *the current study or the present study* to distinguish their own from the others mentioned in the literature review. (Be careful NOT to use these words in your own literature review except to refer to the study you are either proposing or whose results you are reporting.) Notice what issues of methodology the authors highlight in the introduction. They may try to distinguish the special nature of a control group, the elimination of a confound (an uncontrolled variable) they have discovered in previous studies similar to their own, or some innovation they are contributing.

Exercise 7

Copy the phrases or sentences found toward the end of the introduction that signal information about methodology. Search only in Introduction sections, not Method sections.

1. We modified the standard procedure for measuring shoe-size variability by presenting . . .

2. Because the ranking procedures used by Smith (1989) favored women, we offset this bias by . . .

3. Participants were required to read vignettes varying in degree of . . .

4. _____

   _____

5. _____

   _____

6. _____

   _____

The final few paragraphs should also define variables and indicate how you have operationalized your definitions. This applies to both dependent and independent variables. You may have used an established procedure, or you may need to explain briefly your own method.

Exercise 8

Find and copy examples of definitions of variables.

1. Babies were classified according to thumb-sucking categories using the thumb-sketch method.

2. Sense of humor was measured by Curly and Moe's (1968) Laugh Scale.

3. Attractiveness was measured by participants' ratings of the photographs on a 9-point scale.

4. _____

   _____

5. _____

   _____

6. _____

   _____

Literature Review

Before we begin this section, let's take the opportunity to notice that a literature review can be published as such, and there are journals devoted to literature reviews, such as *Review of General Psychology, Psychological Review,* and *Psychological Bulletin.* Students are often asked to write papers based on library research rather than on laboratory research, and these are also literature reviews. A section at the end of this chapter is devoted to this type of review.

Finding the Literature to Review

When you prepare a literature review either for its own sake or as part of the introduction to a research report, you will first want to consult an electronic database through your university library's online resources, and most psychologists start with PsycINFO. Recall the difference between you and the laypeople that I stressed in Chapter 1. Your new professional persona requires that you use only certain types of sources for your literature review: peer-reviewed sources. Peer review means that two or three other scholars in the field have read the work and recommended publication. You cannot generally cite items from the popular press, and many Internet sources are not appropriate. The Internet sometimes does contain suitable sources, but doing a Google or Yahoo search is likely to waste your time. If you do not believe that, stop right now and do a Google search for *healthy aging.* The first page of my search turned up an opportunity to purchase a new balanced fruit drink, become a member of the AARP, learn more about Centrum, and provide managed care for my dad. Incidentally, I could also find links to scholarly articles about Alzheimer's disease and predictors of high intellectual functioning in a group of centenarians. I could have spent the same time checking PsycINFO and been assured that all articles, book chapters, and books from this database are legitimate sources for a psychology paper.

Does this mean that surfing the Internet is of no use to you? Not at all. The first thing you can do is use it to get a better perspective on the range of possibilities for your topic and perhaps narrow it down. You can try looking up some keywords in concept clustering search engines such as www.accumo.com, www.clusty.com, or www.bing.com. If you have a general idea that interests you, you can go to the American Psychological Association website (www.APA.org) and search some keywords to get ideas. For example, I just searched for *adolescent self-esteem* and found 178 documents including some on aggression, anorexia, gay and lesbian parenting, plastic surgery, HIV, bullying, and cognitive therapy. I would not even have to read them to get an idea that might lead to a suitably narrow literature review related to self-esteem.

It is a good idea to become familiar with Boolean search logic. Efficiently using "and," "or," and "not" in your searches will save you time and gain you more relevant sources on all search engines. Try http://www.internettutorials.net/boolean.asp for more details. The staff in your own college or university library will also be happy to help you learn Boolean search logic. Also be sure to use a "wild card" character. It works like this: Suppose you use the keyword *adolescent.* You will miss sources that have the word *adolescence.* If you type *adolesc**, you will get all words that start with those letters, including *adolescent, adolescents,* and *adolescence.*

If you are planning to surf the Internet (and not just PsycINFO), you have to plan to evaluate the sites that seem useful to you. You must be sure that the source is scholarly. It must have an author, a bibliography or reference list, and a date of publication. Look for a publisher that makes sense. You can truncate back the URL to get an idea of the source—go to the address box and delete characters starting from the far right. Stop at each slash, leaving the slash. Press Enter and see what you have. Repeat the process until you get to the domain name. The domain name will end in edu, org, com, net, us, gov, or a country code. If you end up at a magazine or newspaper (e.g., www.nytimes.com), it is not a good source for you, but it may contain a reference to something you can use. It may be a news story about recent research on your topic. Read the item and see whether you can trace the original scholarly publication through PsycINFO.

It is a good general rule that the domains edu, org, and gov are more likely to contain something scholarly than the "dot com" sites. The second rule to follow, as mentioned above, is that your sources should be peer-reviewed. More and more, some very legitimate scholarly sources are available on the Internet. For example, this site contains full-text free peer-reviewed journals: http://www.doaj.org/

Many students like to consult Wikipedia.org. Wikipedia is a site that allows any user to edit and update or create an entry. *Any user.* That could be the person sitting next to you in class or on the bus. I would prefer to trust a psychology textbook to define a term and give me ideas on how to narrow it down for a paper. Don't run the risk of using Wikipedia.com as a reference on a psychology paper or as a source of information that you choose not to reference.

My own effort to find sites on searching the Internet and evaluating Internet sources led me to the following websites that I recommend if you want further help:

http://www.library.jhu.edu/researchhelp/general/evaluating

http://www.internettutorials.net

http://www.lib.berkeley.edu/TeachingLib/Guides/Internet/Evaluate.html

Ultimately, you will end up at a professional abstract retrieval database such as PsycINFO. You will do a keyword search and read many abstracts before deciding which articles to look at for information relevant to your topic. Do not just arbitrarily select the first 20 (or whatever number your professor stipulates) for your paper. You want the best 20, the ones that fit together to make a complete picture of your narrow topic. You will have to read many more abstracts than that to get a feel for what you need. You might get 400 hits and be unable to narrow down your search. Start reading. You will find some articles that are far from your topic. Revise the search with "not" to reduce the number. For example, you might not be interested in therapy, or in depression, or in neuro* articles. Your interest in adolescent self-esteem might have a completely different focus. Knock out all irrelevant items by revising the search at this time to exclude them.

You are looking for theories about your topic, findings relevant to your topic, methodology used to study your topic, and literature reviews about your topic. You will not be able to locate all of the sources you would like to read in your library or through your library's full-text databases. If you have the time, you might want to use interlibrary loan. But at some point, you will say, "Enough!" And you will read and take notes on articles to which you do have access. (Please do take notes. Hot pink highlighting provides a certain aesthetic pleasure, but when it is time to begin writing a paper, notes are much more useful than a stack of articles.)

Annotated Bibliography

One way to take notes is to construct an annotated bibliography. Some professors require annotated bibliographies as freestanding course assignments, and others require them as a preliminary to turning in a literature review paper. If you are not required to produce one, let's start with the premise that those professors might be onto something. What is an annotated bibliography?

Although format and length may vary according to the assignment, the purpose is to summarize and evaluate a source. In the case of research articles in psychology, a useful approach would be to start with the correct APA citation format (see Chapter 8). Then provide the following information:

Purpose of the study

Major theoretical underpinnings

Rationale for hypotheses

Type of sample (not size)

Brief summary of the method

Most important results

Relevance to your work

You can see how approaching note-taking from this perspective can be useful. You will later be able to group studies according to sample or method. You may be able to see that a certain theory is very popular with many of your authors. You may find conflicting results. If you are really lucky, you will sense how your own paper should be organized.

Writing the Review

For a research report, the rule given by the *Publication Manual* says, "Discuss the relevant related literature but do not feel compelled to include an exhaustive historical account" (p. 28). Students, however, are usually held to a different standard: They will need to communicate to their instructor that they have read *and understood* other research articles in the related area. To do this, they often need to provide more detail about the studies they review than do authors of the studies reviewed. You can still be selective about what *kind* of detail you provide.

Each study cited in your literature review is cited for a specific purpose. For example, you may want to stress method in one and findings in another. You should not summarize exhaustively every study in your review. However, you will need to provide a paragraph or two on those studies even though the published articles offer only a sentence or two about relevant research studies.

When you attempt to summarize the method of a published study that contains several conditions or several similar experiments with small variations, concentrate on one experiment or condition and describe it clearly. Then you will be able to mention the variations very briefly, and they will be clear (Bem, 1995). For example, for a vignette study, you might describe one of the vignettes and then explain that the other groups read vignettes that varied the age of the protagonist or the number of years of experience of the fictional job applicant. For a study of instructional methods, describe one method, the tasks, and the dependent measure. Then you can briefly note that other groups were identical except for the instructional methods, which you then describe.

It is not usually desirable to note that several experiments were reported and then to describe each one. Describe the general method only. Then, as with the description of various groups, you can explain how the variations on the method were accomplished. When you describe results after using this technique for describing the method, you will find it easy to compare the results for each group or experimental variation at the end of your paragraph.

After gathering all your notes, it is time to organize them for the review. Keep in mind the point you are making about each study. This will help you introduce the paragraph containing the details. There should be some evidence of linear logic in the introduction, but students sometimes find themselves without good reasons for sequencing a particular set of studies. When this happens, they introduce paragraphs with phrases such as "Smith (1995) found that . . ." or "Smith (1995) also did a study of . . ." But this type of writing introduces a common problem: failing to show the connections among the studies in the review. Thus, *also* is not always a good term to link studies together. But you might want to make the point that the two researchers did something very similar. Perhaps you have decided to build a case for someone's theory by adding more evidence. If this is true, then say so. Alternatively, you might prefer to emphasize that this study appears similar to another, but an important difference remains, and you want to explain it. Knowing *why* you are including a particular study will give you a much better idea of *where* to include it. In this way, your paragraphs will begin with more natural transitions and have appropriately clear topic sentences. Once again, keep in mind that your own literature review will contain more details than there are in the articles you read. Now it is time to take a look at these types of transitions.

Exercise 9

Copy phrases that introduce the discussion of specific studies under review. Look particularly for words or phrases that serve as markers for the author's organizational plan.

1. In line with these findings . . .

2. Another puzzling aspect of memory is . . .

3. Although Smith's (2009) findings are clear and consistent, Jones (2010) has pointed out . . .

4. The results of *x* are consistent with *y*.

5. Smith (1995) developed a system for classifying aspects of the phenomenon identified by Jones (1994).

6. According to Smith (2011), children who have the strongest attachments to their pets . . .

7. Another kind of research tactic has been to . . .

8. _____

9. _____

10. _____

11. _____

12. _____

Your literature review is not the place for your opinions. If you find the sample in an experiment to be very small, you can call attention to that fact only if someone else has found different results with a similar but larger sample. Perhaps the author has noted a problem in his or her own Discussion section; if so, you then have tacit permission to cite the author's own misgivings. You may speculate about contradictory findings, but once again, be careful not to be disparaging of the work of either author. Try not to write about what authors did not do unless you are contrasting it with what you are about to do or with what someone else did. For example, Smith might not have tested middle-aged adults; Jones might not have had a no-treatment control group. You may not mention this just to show off the fact that you noticed it. If your study contains middle-aged participants, then you can use Smith's results (emphasizing the missing middle-aged group) to provide a rationale for your own hypotheses or design.

Do not forget the rules on verb tense in your literature review. You are reporting on work that has been completed. Therefore, use past tense (*found*) or present perfect (*have found*). Even your own work has already been completed by the time you report the results. So use past tense when you talk about the purpose of your study, the hypotheses, or what the participants had to do. The exception is when your introduction concerns a research *proposal*. Students are often required to write introductions for this purpose, and in this case, the research is clearly not completed. For research proposals, use present and future tense in writing about your study (e.g., "the purpose is," and "the participants will").

▲ REMINDER BOX ▼

Use past tense to describe research findings—your own and those covered in your literature review.

The literature review may require the use of headings. The overall heading for the introduction is not used, but sometimes subheadings can be. When you just cannot think of a good transition sentence for your next paragraph, it may be time to consider breaking your review into sections. If you have a heading for a section, you can avoid that difficult transition sentence; the heading tells the reader where you are going. But don't abuse the help of headings. For example, don't use headings to avoid logical sequencing. Use them to enhance the evidence of your logic.

Here is where an outline will help you. Although everyone is taught that it is appropriate to outline a paper before writing it, some people just do not do so. You may find, however, that it is easier to outline your paper *after* you begin to write. Try an outline (if you have not used headings) when you finish your first draft. Most people do better with a printed draft rather than with an on-screen manuscript. Outline the paper as it stands. If this proves difficult, you have not done a good job of organizing your paper. The topic sentences should guide you in your outline. If they are missing, this is the time for you to provide them. Outline again after your second draft. If you still cannot do it, ask someone else to try it, and if that person also finds it difficult to outline, ask why. A good literature review should be easy to outline.

▲ REMINDER BOX ▼

Try to outline your paper after it is written.

The *Publication Manual* is very explicit about how to organize your manuscript with headings. (Headings are especially useful in the Method section, and we will take them up again in Chapter 4.) A manuscript may have headings and subheadings. The subheadings may have subheadings of their own, and so on. These are referred to as *levels* of headings. Students' work is likely to have one, two, or three levels of headings. If you have one level, it means that none of your sections has a subsection. These headings should be centered, boldface, with important words capitalized.

Here Is an Example of Such a Heading

If you have two levels, it means that your sections have subsections. Your big units are headed as above, bold, centered, and containing uppercase and lowercase letters. Your subheadings are also in uppercase and lowercase letters, but they are up against the left margin and bold. They look like this:

Here Is the Main Heading

Here Is the Subheading

Here is the beginning of the paragraph you will write under this subheading.

Finally, if you have three levels, that is, if your subsections have subsections, it begins the same way. But your lowest level is boldface, is indented with your paragraph, and has only the first word capitalized. It ends with a period:

Here Is the Main Heading (Call it A)

Here Is the Subheading for That Section (Call it B)

And here is the heading under that (call it C). This is the material that you will write in Section C.

When you are finished writing this material, you can start a new section with a heading like C. When that is finished you may wish to do another, or else you can go back to the level above it—B. You are even allowed to have another big section start with the type of heading I've called A. However, follow the outline rules you already know: If you introduce a new level, be sure to have at least two subsections at that level. Believe it or not, the *Publication Manual* will take you through steps allowing you to use up to five levels. But don't try this at home.

A Few Additional Things to Think About When the Literature R eview Is the Paper

It is not uncommon for students to prepare theoretical or practical literature reviews (or both). Of course, you will not want to include hypotheses or statements about your methodology if the review itself is the body of your paper. You can identify this type of article in a journal in one of several ways. First, you can notice that there is no Method or

Results section. Second, the table of contents of the journal often breaks down the contents into sections. Look for articles that are not in the section called "Research." Finally, you can go straight to a journal that is devoted entirely to review articles, such as *Current Directions in Psychological Science* or *Psychological Bulletin*. These sorts of reviews can take several forms. You might find an article that is an attempt to provide the current state of the art on a topic—one that summarizes the most up-to-date and methodologically sound research on a topic. Some journals publish reviews that are more evaluative, reviewing the literature to make a case for a specific theory, and these could even be called theoretical articles. Also, there is a statistical method called meta-analysis that brings the findings of many different empirical studies together in one analysis. Articles of this type are also literature reviews but with an emphasis on developing a statistical summary of the literature.

The opening sentence of the review resembles the opening sections you have studied. But the purpose will be different. The title may convey important information about the purpose of the review. The abstract often contains this information. In addition, you might find a statement of purpose in the concluding paragraphs of the article.

Exercise 10

Find some review articles and copy the purpose.

> *Look in the second paragraph and find the purpose of this one (or find an article of your own):* Raine, A. (2002). Biosocial studies of antisocial and violent behavior in children and adults: A review. *Journal of Abnormal Child Psychology, 30,* 311–326.

1. _____

   _____

> *Look in the fifth paragraph for the purpose of this one (or find an article of your own):* Finkel, E. J., & Eastwick, P. W. (2008). Speed-dating. *Current Directions in Psychological Science, 17,* 193–197.

2. _____

   _____

   _____

It is very difficult to organize a review paper because each topic presents idiosyncratic problems for the writer. In many ways, it is easier to organize a paper on the basis of your original research because the organizational structure is restricted by APA's own formula. Whether you are experienced with writing literature reviews or new to it, organizing the paper is always the most challenging part. But even though it seems as if each topic requires its own unique organization, it can still be instructive to see how others have handled this problem with their topics. If you scan a number of articles from *Current Directions in Psychological Science* or *Psychological Bulletin*, you will begin to see patterns that can help you.

Most reviews start with an introduction of their own, consisting of two to three paragraphs. This introduction, like that of the empirical research report, sets the context for the work: why this is an important issue, what sorts of people and how many have these problems or concerns, what public policy and/or practice issues are affected by this problem. The thing to be careful of here, as was noted before, is not to underestimate the expertise of your audience. Assume that they know that America is graying at a fast pace, that drugs are a problem in our high schools, and that in some settings, therapists are burdened with a heavy caseload. Be very specific with your demographic information— restrict your context material to the narrow population that you are studying. And then get on with the show.

You wish to make a point with your review. You have an original contribution to make even if you have not done empirical research, because you have gained an original insight or perspective from your reading of the literature. That is why someone is going to rely on your work to gain a secondhand appreciation for what is out there. If you know where all this is going, you will have an easier time with the organization. Do not give in to the temptation to go through your material chronologically unless you have decided that historical perspective is necessary for the reader to get your point. Usually, your point is that one way of looking at a psychological issue is the one you favor. That is an excellent start. How will you convince the reader? You will have to organize the studies in your review accordingly. But do not forget your obligation to present both sides of an issue fairly, noting which studies support each.

One good method is to organize around competing theoretical models (Bem, 1995). Some studies support one theory or model, and some studies support another. Sometimes there are three or four models. If you think of your readings in these terms, then you will be likely to end by making a point about which model seems to be the most reasonable, given the evidence for it. Many reviews end with suggestions for future research. But beware of ending with details for methodological improvements. Suggestions for further research as a final statement are best when they cover broad areas because the review itself covers a topic exhaustively and the reviewer is in a position to see where large gaps in our knowledge may be. It can be interesting to end with something more memorable than suggestions for future research. This is a good place for bringing home your point of view in a more general way (Bem, 1995).

Looking Back and Looking Ahead

In this chapter, you have studied the major components of the Introduction section: literature review, purpose of the study, theoretical implications, definitions of variables, and hypotheses with rationales. Although much of this is formulaic and fairly simple to model, the literature review is more challenging. It is the largest section and the most variable.

The key to writing a good literature review is doing a good literature search. Search exhaustively in the professional literature even if your project is relatively small. Try to get the most relevant articles in your possession, whatever the number of references will ultimately be. After becoming *very* familiar with them and taking notes on them (perhaps in the form of an annotated bibliography), you may find that an organization of the material becomes obvious to you. If not, think about which theoretical frameworks they rely on, what methodological similarities and differences you find, and what implications they present in their Discussion sections. Develop your subtopics from these areas.

The next chapter is about preparing the Method section. This section is fairly standardized, and you will find it easy to write. The main thing to keep in mind is that your reader needs to judge your work on the basis of his or her understanding of what you did. Be very explicit and very patient. Do not leave anything to the reader's imagination.

For more information:

Topic	Publication Manual	Concise Rules
Introduction in general	2.05	—
Verb tense	3.06, 3.18	1.06, 1.18
Levels of heading	3.03	1.03

CHAPTER 4

Preparing the Method Section

The purpose of the Method section is twofold. First, by providing the details of the sample and procedures, you make it possible for other researchers to replicate your study exactly or to make explicit how they are deviating from your procedure. Second, after a reader knows the details of your method, it becomes possible to judge the reliability and validity of your experiment. Once you understand these joint purposes, you will be able to make decisions more easily about the level of detail you must achieve.

Note about the sixth edition of the *Publication Manual*: Starting with this edition, authors are invited to use a supplemental website for their articles where more detailed information can be provided. Some of this detail is the sort that previously would have been in an appendix or unavailable except by corresponding with the author. However, appendixes are still available for this purpose. An appendix might contain stimulus materials, description of equipment, or detailed demographic information for participants. Web-based, online supplemental archives are suggested when direct download might be desirable (e.g., lengthy computer code), when the print format is inappropriate (e.g., video clips), when few readers would require the information (e.g., detailed intervention protocols), and when the print format would be expensive or unwieldy (e.g., color figures or oversized tables).

Organization

It is common for the Method section to be divided into subsections. These will generally include at least *Participants* (or *Subjects*) and *Procedure.* Often, the *Materials, Apparatus, Measures,* or *Stimuli* will be subsections of the Method section as well. Beginning with the 6th edition of the *Publication Manual* they are more likely to be lower-level subsections of the Procedure subsection. When archival data are used (data files that already exist—that is, you did not need to recruit participants to provide data), you may see *Sample* as a subheading instead of *Participants.* The Method section will also contain important information about the research design, for example, how conditions were manipulated, how behavior was measured or observed, how participants were assigned to conditions, and whether it was a within- or between-subjects design. You are free to decide how subsections can best clarify your own work.

Exercise 1

Look at some research articles and copy the subheadings from the Method section. Note that in editions of the *Publication Manual* prior to the fourth (1994), the word *subject* was used instead of *participant.* In the 4th and 5th edition, *participants* was clearly favored. The advice in the sixth edition (2010) is to choose the term that is in common use in one's subfield. Therefore, you may find a section called *Subjects* or *Participants* or *Sample.* You will be safe if you use *participants* unless your group did not provide direct consent, as when you observe people engaged in some public activity.

1. Participants
   Materials
   Design and Procedure

2. Subjects
   Procedures
   Measures

3. _____

   _____

   _____

4. _____

_____

_____

5. _____

_____

_____

▲ REMINDER BOX ▼

The titles for the subsections of the Method section are flexible. Use them to your advantage.

Now let's consider the contents of some of these subsections.

Participants

Only the rules for human research subjects will be considered at this time. Students more often report research with human subjects than with animal subjects, but be advised that the *Publication Manual* does explain how to describe animal subjects, and that will be discussed later.

▲ REMINDER BOX ▼

People are usually participants; other animals are always subjects.

Assuming, then, that you are describing human beings who provided data for an experiment, first indicate how many people participated. You must also provide some standard information about them and whatever information is relevant to your particular study. The most basic level of information about participants is age and sex. Report age ranges and means. Elsewhere in your manuscript, standard deviations accompany all means, but this is not the convention for reporting the ages of participants. However, do indicate the appropriate unit of measure (e.g., years, months). If you have more than one group of participants, you do not have to report ages for each group unless the groups vary notably or intentionally. But you do have to indicate how many participants were in each group.

▲ REMINDER BOX ▼

Report age ranges and mean age of participants. Indicate the unit of measure.

Report how many men (or boys) and women (or girls) there were. The *Publication Manual* cautions against the use of the terms *male* and *female* as nouns. You should use *men* and *women* and *girls* and *boys* (high school age and younger) instead. You can use *females* and *males* if the age range includes both children and adults. Otherwise, use *female* and *male* only as adjectives (e.g., male experimenter, female clients, female and male adolescents). Other ways to reduce gender bias include the following:

> Use *same sex* and *other sex* rather than *same sex* and *opposite sex*.
>
> Use *people* or *humankind* rather than *mankind*.

Don't always write *men and women*. Sometimes write *women and men*. (Avoid placing the socially dominant group first.)

▲ REMINDER BOX ▼

Use *men* and *women* instead of *males* and *females*.

Exercise 2

Copy sentences from the Participants or Subjects subsections of research articles that indicate the number, age, and sex of participants.

1. One hundred women aged 35 to 55 years (*M* age = 40.11 years) participated.

2. Participants were 32 undergraduates at the University of X (18 women and 14 men, *M* age = 19.73 years).

3. The sample consisted of 17 male and 18 female research scientists and their spouses. They ranged in age from 40 to 65 years (*M* = 50.17).

4. _____

_____

5. _____

_____

6. _____

_____

It is also appropriate when possible to specify the race or ethnicity of participants. The *Publication Manual* is specific with regard to which designations are preferred (e.g., *Asian* or *Asian American* rather than *Oriental; Native American* rather than *American Indian,* but in many cases the specific Indian group or nation would be best). Remember that racial and ethnic group labels are proper nouns and should be capitalized (e.g., *Black* and *White).* Avoid *non-White.* It implies that White is the standard, and it is also imprecise. Always be sensitive to the changing standards for inoffensive labeling. You can ask your participants about their preferred designations if you are unsure. And remember that "hyphenated Americans" really have no hyphens in their spelling: Cuban American, African American, Asian American. This rule holds even if the labels are used together as a single modifier, for example, Irish American psychiatrists.

▲ REMINDER BOX ▼

Racial and ethnic group labels are proper nouns. Capitalize them.

Consider the information that will be needed for readers to generalize from your sample to a population. Often educational level is indicated. Provide characteristics which may limit generalization (e.g., participants may be students in psychology classes at a Midwestern university or patients in a Boston hospital).

Avoiding bias is important in many types of description:

■   For sexual orientation, preferred terms are *lesbian women, gay men,* and *bisexual women* or *bisexual men.* Avoid the term *homosexual* and specify gender.

■   Do not reduce people to their diagnoses. It is better to say *people with bipolar disorder* than to call them *bipolars.*

■   Likewise, literally put the person before the disability: *Child with autism* is better than *autistic child.*

■   Avoid language that suggests helplessness: *People who reported being sexually abused as teenagers* is preferable to *teen-age victims of sexual abuse.* People are not *confined* to wheelchairs. They *use* wheelchairs.

Do not use *elderly* as a noun; substitute *older adults* or *older persons.*

Exercise 3

Copy sentences or phrases that indicate demographic characteristics of the sample that seem to be included for information purposes, not because of special selection by the researcher. Think about why the author reported this information (usually to indicate limits of generalizability).

1. One hundred women . . . living in rural communities in West Virginia agreed to participate.

2. The participants were 435 college students who completed an anonymous questionnaire and were paid $435.

3. All children were of middle to upper-middle socioeconomic status.

4. _____

_____

5. _____

_____

6. _____

_____

Often, participants in research studies come from specific populations relevant to the nature of the study. You may have used selection criteria: for example, marital status, diagnosis, or sexual orientation. They may be children at certain grade levels, infants born full term, patients with specific diagnoses, children whose parents are divorced, people with specific test score ranges, people above a certain educational level, and so on. Some of the subfields of psychology operate with conventions of their own. For example, clinical research often contains diagnostic labels for participants; infant research may include minimum APGAR scores and/or minimum birth weights; older adult samples may include educational level and/or verbal test scores.

Exercise 4

Copy examples of participants that seem to indicate selection criteria. As you do this, think about why these characteristics were selected by the researchers.

1. . . . who reported normal speech and hearing.

2. Participants were undergraduates who were not currently enrolled in a yoga class.

3. Participants were identical twins born less than 1 month prematurely.

4. _____

   _____

5. _____

   _____

6. _____

   _____

Note how participants were selected. Perhaps they volunteered, answered an advertisement, or were stopped on the street. Do not say that they were "randomly selected" unless they really were. That would mean that you had access to the whole population (of university students, patients at the hospital, or people on the street) and actually used a technique to select randomly (e.g., a coin toss, a table of random numbers, or numbers pulled out of a hat) the people you solicited to participate.

▲ **REMINDER BOX** ▼

Do not say "participants were randomly selected" when "participants volunteered" is more accurate.

Sometimes people are given incentives for their participation in experiments. Undergraduate psychology students may get extra credit or may participate as one way to fulfill course requirements. People may be paid to participate. You must indicate what, if anything, was given to participants in exchange for their help with the experiment. Otherwise, you may just say that they volunteered to participate.

After you have made relevant information about participants clear to the reader, begin to use those more descriptive terms instead of referring to them as *participants* (e.g., the young and older adults, the children, the students, the physicians). Alternatively, you can use terms that describe the nature of their participation (e.g., respondents, perceivers, raters).

Sometimes participants are randomly assigned to groups; at other times, the grouping factor is based on some characteristic of the participants (e.g., age, sex, occupation, nationality, diagnosis). If the groupings are based on participant characteristics, describe the details of this grouping in the Participants section. By the way, do not say, "Participants were divided into men and women." This sentence is a notorious annoyance to professors. If you randomly assigned participants to groups, it is usually more appropriate to indicate that you did so in your Procedure subsection.

Exercise 5

Copy sentences that indicate that participants were grouped according to subject characteristics.

> *You will find an interesting one here (or choose your own):* Wenzel, A., Barth, T. C., & Holt, C. S. (2003). Thought suppression in spider-fearful and nonfearful individuals. *The Journal of General Psychology, 130,* 191–205.

1. There were 28 speed daters and 13 speed skaters.

2. The sample was composed of 100 meat packers who either (a) were still employed at the time of the experiment ($n = 30$), (b) had left voluntarily ($n = 30$), or (c) had been fired ($n = 40$).

3. _____

   _____

4. _____

_____

5. _____

_____

When participants are not randomly assigned to groups and are grouped instead by inherent characteristics, the groups may differ from each other in undesirable ways as well. For example, a divorced group may be older than a nondivorced group, or an older-adult group may have completed fewer years of school than a middle-aged group. When it is relevant to the research to demonstrate that these other variables have been controlled or that differences have been noted, a researcher includes a statistical analysis of these group differences in the Participants section. Thus, in this section, you may find descriptive statistics and/or statistical comparisons of means of such variables as age, education, general health, or verbal ability.

▲ REMINDER BOX ▼

Statistics may be reported in the Participants subsection if they describe preexisting differences (or similarities) between groups.

When some participants do not complete the research tasks (attrition), it is necessary to indicate how many dropped out and why. Some percentage of infants gets fussy; some adults do not come back for a second session; some people may not meet certain criteria after testing has begun. When surveys are mailed to participants, some surveys are not returned. Indicate what percentage of surveys was actually completed. When participants do not complete the study, avoid saying that they *failed* to do so. Say that they *did not* do so.

Exercise 6

Copy sentences that refer to dropouts from experiments or survey return rates.

> ***You will find some fussy babies here (or choose something of your own):*** Miller, J. L., Ables, E. M., King, A. P., & West, M. J. (2009). Different patterns of contingent stimulation differentially affect attention span in prelinguistic infants. *Infant Behavior and Development, 32,* 254–261.

1. We excluded data from nine additional students because they had previously been in a bungee-jumping experiment.
2. Of the initial 300 participants, 45 did not appear for follow-up testing. Data from these participants are not included in any of the analyses.

3. _____

_____

4. _____

_____

Power

Indicate in the Participants section how the sample size was determined. Usually, this will involve a power analysis indicating that with the given sample size, the analysis for the main hypothesis had sufficient power to find an effect if one was present. A typical way to construct this sentence is as follows:

For the main analysis, this sample size provided a power of .8 to detect a medium effect.

Ethical Treatment

If you have come this far in your study of psychological science, then you are familiar with the APA Ethics Code. When you prepare your research report you must certify that you have adhered to those standards in the treatment of your participants. Currently, the *Publication Manual* encourages authors to indicate their compliance in the Participants section. Additionally, authors are required to attest to its truth in the cover letters they submit with their manuscripts. This requirement would appear in the instructions to authors printed somewhere in the journals. In the past, this statement might not have appeared in every case in the Participants section. Compliance with these guidelines would be assumed for all studies published in those journals.

A Few Words About Animals

When nonhuman animals are research subjects, the *Publication Manual* provides additional guidance. You must report the genus, species, and strain number or specific information such as supplier and stock designation. Sex, weight, and physical condition are important. Indicate any special handling that affects replication efforts. As with humans, ethical treatment is assumed, because most APA journals will have their authors stipulate to that in their cover letters. Finally, use neuter pronouns: The rat waited in *its* cage (not *his* cage). Likewise, you will use *that* or *which* and refer to the rat *that* waited in its cage, not the rat *who* waited in its cage. The exception to this neuter gender rule is for those who name their animals, as primate researchers are wont to do. Once you have referred to your chimp as Elvis, you should later refer to *him* rather than *it*.

Procedure

There are two points of view that you must be aware of in this part of the manuscript: the researcher's and the participant's. Use the researcher's point of view to describe how the experiment was organized; use the participant's point of view to describe the task.

Start with the organization. What were the conditions? Did everyone participate in every condition (within-subjects design), or were people grouped in some way (between-groups design)? Were they grouped by some previously noted characteristic or randomly assigned? (Please remember that people are assigned to conditions; conditions are not assigned to people.)

Provide names for your groups or conditions that help the reader to remember the key distinguishing features. The *alcohol-information group* and the *no-information group* are better designations than Group A and Group B. Feel free to give a short name or abbreviation to a group after describing it. For example, the alcohol-information group might be the AI group, and the no-information group might be the NI group. If you can make it even easier for the reader, do so: ALC group and No-ALC group. Be sure to refer to the group consistently by that term in the rest of the manuscript. Note that the names of groups and conditions are not capitalized unless they have been given letter or number names (*Group A* but *alcohol-information group*). Usually, however, the abbreviations are written in all uppercase letters. Don't overdo abbreviations. If the reader is more confused than helped by a complex set of abbreviations, just use the entire words as labels.

▲ REMINDER BOX ▼
Capitalize the name of the condition only if the name is a letter or includes a number.

A description of an experimental manipulation often includes a summary of the instructions to participants. If the instructions were important in the manipulation, provide them verbatim in the text or in an appendix or online supplement. If an intervention was carried out, it would be important to know the setting, some information about the person who carried it out, the duration, and the number of sessions. Explain whether the participants were seen individually or in groups of an indicated size.

Exercise 7

Copy sentences from articles that include information about conditions or groups.

1. Half of the participants were randomly assigned to meet in face-to-face groups (FTF), and the other half watched videotapes (VT).

2. Participants were randomly assigned to one of the conditions of the 2 (letter: accurate vs. inaccurate) × 2 (hiring decision: favorable vs. unfavorable) factorial design.

3. Each participant saw one of the three taped sporting events.

4. _____

   _____

5. _____

   _____

Be careful with the terms *group* and *condition*. They are related and almost equivalent in the researcher's mind, but they are not linguistically equivalent. People can be in groups; they cannot be in conditions. Groups can perform tasks, but conditions cannot. It is often best to use participants as sentence subjects. For example, "Depending on condition, participants were told that they would hear A or see B."

▲ **REMINDER BOX** ▼

Use the term *condition* carefully. People are assigned to conditions, not the other way around. People cannot be in conditions, and conditions cannot perform tasks.

Once you have explained how the experiment was organized, explain the task. Start with the general nature of the task, and then give details that apply to all of the groups. Later, explain how the groups differed. Use the participant as the focus rather than the experimenter. That is, say that the participants read, rated, completed, listened to, or watched. This is preferable to saying that the experimenter gave the participant something to read, rate, complete, listen to, or watch.

Exercise 8

From Procedure subsections, copy examples of tasks that participants perform.

1. Each participant was required to drink two beverages.
2. Participants were led to believe that a student was conducting a study of teacher ratings. They read that . . .
3. Participants labeled each photograph with the adjectives that seemed to describe the person in that photograph best.

4. _____

   _____

5. _____

   _____

6. _____

   _____

Explain the method of scoring only if it is not obvious. Thus, an answer of 3 on a 5-point scale will be understood to be scored as 3. But in a tracing task, you should mention whether an error was scored when the tracer's mark touched the pattern or went over the guideline. Was it another error when it came back in? If a summary score was calculated and used for data analysis, explain how that was done and refer back to the appropriate term in the hypotheses.

Apparatus

Include this subsection only if you have used special equipment. You must make clear what a research participant using this equipment actually *does*. It is often difficult for students to decide on an appropriate level of detail for a piece of equipment. There are two goals to keep in mind. The first is to allow readers to understand the experiment from the point of view of the participant. The second is to provide enough detail to allow replication of the experiment. When you describe the function of the equipment from the participant's point of view, concentrate on the task and the special nature of the equipment that facilitates it. For example, if you have a mirror-tracing device, you need to mention that it is designed to allow someone to write with a pencil while looking only at the reflection of this action in a mirror. It is not appropriate to indicate how this looks from the experimenter's viewpoint or how difficult it is to set up.

▲ REMINDER BOX ▼

Describe devices from the point of view of the participant, not the experimenter.

If the device is available for purchase, provide the name of the company and the make and model number. If it is a computer, indicate what type. Computer programs may be described here if you are also describing anything about the computer itself or the keyboard. Otherwise, programs are often listed in the Materials subsection. If you have constructed a piece of equipment, describe its function in detail. When you identify the parts of your apparatus, keep in mind that you must refer to these parts in a consistent way throughout your manuscript (e.g., the "red button" cannot later be called the "red key"). Remember to use metric units when giving details of size.

You may use a diagram or a photograph if that would make it easier for the reader to understand. For this, follow the rules for *figures* (see Chapter 5). If necessary, you may use an appendix to describe equipment you have constructed. As a general rule, when you have constructed a device, make clear in the text whatever is necessary for the reader to judge your work; include an appendix with additional detail only for those who wish to construct a similar device for purposes of replication. You do not need to describe ordinary furniture or its layout, stopwatches, or room dividers.

Exercise 9

List items you find in the Apparatus subsection of articles. Indicate whether the item was purchased, constructed, or a modified version of something purchased. You might have better luck with this exercise if you use journals describing infant research or research with nonhuman subjects.

> *Find out how fast cuttlefish learn that prawns in a clear plastic tube are not worth attacking:* Purdy, J. E., Dixon, D., Estrada, A., Peters, A., Riedlinger, E., & Suarez, R. (2006). Prawn-in-a-tube procedure: Habituation or associative learning in cuttlefish? *The Journal of General Psychology, 133,* 131–152.

1. Experimental chambers (constructed) . . .

2. Sessions were recorded by means of a Panasonic camcorder (purchased).

3. _____

4. _____

Materials

Materials in this sense usually refers to printed materials. These may also be called *stimuli.* Audios, videos, and computer programs are sometimes included as well. The same rules apply here as for the previous subsection: Allow readers to understand the task from the point of view of the participants while also providing enough information for replication. Likewise, in this subsection, you may be using materials bought or borrowed (with appropriate citations) from other authors, or you may have constructed them yourself.

When you have used published tests or questionnaires, it is usually easy to list them in the Materials subsection. Give the author and year, as you would for any citation. Indicate what the test measures. Try to tie the terms to your Introduction section, in which you have noted how you operationalized your dependent measures (e.g., Jones and Smith's [1965] Warmth Test was used to measure empathy). If you have reliability and validity information that pertains to your population, include those references as well. Provide evidence of cultural validity. Do not forget to give a brief description of the task or the items (you can provide sample items) from the point of view of the participant. State the meaning of the score (e.g., scores range from 15 to 45, with higher scores indicating higher levels of empathy). Use the past tense to describe what your participants did (e.g., the children placed a mark . . .) and the present tense to describe enduring characteristics of a test (e.g., the test measures . . .; high scores indicate . . .).

Questionnaires and tests that you devise yourself should be explained more fully. In addition to all of the information suggested for published tests, it is helpful to provide sample questions in the body of the paper and the complete test or questionnaire in the form of an appendix or online supplement. Researchers often construct scales that require participants to choose a numerical response, for example, from 1 to 5. These may be referred to as Likert scales or Likert-type scales. The high and low points (1 and 5 in the current example) are called the *anchors* of the scale. There are two points of punctuation to learn about scales: There is a hyphen between the number and the word *point* (e.g., 5-point scale), and the anchors are italicized. Usually, the points between the anchors are not labeled, but if they are, these labels must also be noted and italicized.

▲ REMINDER BOX ▼

Italicize the anchors of a scale.

Exercise 10

Find examples of descriptions of scales. Copy sentences and phrases that indicate the number of points on the scale and the labels or anchors.

1. Test A uses a 5-point Likert format with responses ranging from 1 *(almost never or never true)* to 5 *(almost always or always true)*.

2. Participants indicated on a 5-point rating scale *(1 = not at all true of me, 5 = very true of me).*

3. Responses range from *not at all true of me* (1) to *totally true of me* (5).

4. _____

   _____

5. _____

   _____

6. _____

   _____

Sometimes researchers use materials or stimuli that are not tests. They may be passages to read, lists to learn, videotapes to watch, diagrams to copy, and so on. As with tests, this type of material may have been developed by others and used as previously designed, developed by others and modified by you, or developed entirely for your experiment. Be sure to indicate the source accordingly. In describing these materials, follow the same rules of explaining the task from the point of view of the participant and giving enough detail for replication (perhaps in an appendix, table, or figure).

It is tricky to describe materials that vary by experimental condition before you have described the actual procedure. If the design and materials are interrelated (e.g., different word lists for different groups, vignettes whose protagonists vary by experimental group), remember that you are under no obligation to have a separate Materials subsection. You can use the label *Design and Materials* if this happens. In that subsection, you explain that there were several groups, how participants were assigned to the groups, and what was (were) the independent variable(s) that controlled the grouping. Then the reader will be ready for the information that each group received slightly different materials. Remember that a reader can become confused when there are several conditions that differ primarily according to the materials used, especially if you describe the materials before describing the conceptual differences among the conditions. Therefore, it may be better not to use a special Materials subsection than to confuse a reader with descriptions of sets of materials for various experimental groups before you have explained the purpose of the groups.

Finally, if your participants were deceived in any way, indicate that they were debriefed at some point in their participation.

Remember Your Audience

When in doubt about what level of detail to use, assume always that your audience is composed of experienced research psychologists. They know:

1. *How to randomize:* Do not explain that you had one hat for men and one for women and that you put each condition label in each hat and pulled one out every time you got ready to test someone. Just say that participants were randomly assigned to conditions or treatment groups. If additional details are relevant (e.g., there were equal numbers of men and women in each group), state them briefly.

2. *The meaning of such terms as counterbalance, control, and being blind to experimental conditions*: Do not say that half of the group randomly got red first and then green and the other half got green first and then red. Just say the order of presentation of the colors was counterbalanced.

3. *How to phrase instructions that stress speed and accuracy:* Do not say that participants were told to read as fast as they could but to try not to make mistakes. Just say that instructions stressed speed and accuracy.

4. *How to create an answer sheet for their own use:* Just say that answers were recorded or responses were recorded verbatim.

5. *When to construct reminders for themselves:* Do not say that the correct answers were written lightly in pencil on the backs of the cards so that the experimenter would know which answers were correct. Say nothing.

6. *How to handle ordinary materials:* Do not explain that participants used pencils to write on their answer sheets and that they gave them to the experimenter when they were finished. Just describe the answer sheets.

▲ REMINDER BOX ▼

Do not tell readers more than they need to know. Assume common sense and familiarity with experimental methodology.

Looking Back and Looking Ahead

In this chapter, you have learned some general rules about writing a Method section and some very picky ones. In general, write so that others can judge the worth of your conclusions. That means that they must know exactly what you did and to whom you did it. A few readers may want to replicate. Do not leave out anything that will mess them up.

You have to provide a good bit of detail about participants; therefore, some of the pickiest rules for this section have to do with avoiding bias and being sensitive in describing people. You want to give men and women equal treatment, conform to race and ethnic labeling practices for the profession, treat sexual orientation without giving offense, and avoid demeaning labels having to do with illness and disability. Do not presume that you already know how these things are done. The APA is full of surprises. Other picky details concern how measures and conditions (groups) are described. Here, watch out for rules about capitalization, use of italics, and hyphenation.

In the next chapter, you may find that APA style gets even more finicky. The Results section is full of mathematical and statistical material that provides many traps for the naïve writer. Use words—use symbols. Use italics—don't. Leave a space—don't leave a space. Use a number—use a word. Use a hyphen—don't. The good news is that there is a rule for every question you might have. Also, there are many standardized sentences that have to be figured out only once and then can be repeated for the rest of your life. The bad news is . . . that there is a rule for every question you might forget to ask.

For more information:

Topic	Publication Manual	Concise Rules
Method section generally	2.06	—
Subsections	2.06	—
Participants versus subjects	3.11 Guideline 3	1.11 Guideline 3
Animals	2.06, 3.20	1.20
Demographics	2.06	—
Ethical treatment	1.11, 8.04	—
Apparatus	2.06	—
Procedure	2.06	—
Gender/sex	3.11 Guideline 1 3.12 and supplemental material at www.apastyle.org	1.11 Guideline 1 1.12 and supplemental material at www.apastyle.org
Stereotypes, Reducing bias in language	3.11 and supplemental material at www.apastyle.org	1.11 and supplemental material at www.apastyle.org
Sensitivity to labels	3.11 Guideline 2 and supplemental material at www.apastyle.org	1.11 Guideline 2 and supplemental material at www.apastyle.org
Sexual orientation	3.13 and supplemental material at www.apastyle.org	1.13 and supplemental material at www.apastyle.org
Racial/ethnic identity	3.14 and supplemental material at www.apastyle.org	1.14 and supplemental material at www.apastyle.org

(continued)

Topic	Publication Manual	Concise Rules
Diagnosis	3.11 Guideline 2 and supplemental material at www.apastyle.org	1.11 Guideline 2 and supplemental material at www.apastyle.org
Disabilities	3.15 and supplemental material at www.apastyle.org	1.15 and supplemental material at www.apastyle.org
Age	3.16 and supplemental material at www.apastyle.org	1.16 and supplemental material at www.apastyle.org
"Failed to participate"	3.11 Guideline 3	1.11 Guideline 3
Metric system	4.39, 4.40 and, for a complete list of abbreviations, supplemental material at www.apastyle.org	4.09, 4.10 and, for a complete list of abbreviations, supplemental material at www.apastyle.org
Anchors of scales/italics	4.07, 4.21	2.08, 3.01
Hyphenation	4.13 and Table 4.1	2.14 and Table 2.1
Appendices and supplemental websites	2.13	6.03, 6.04
Groups and conditions	4.19, 4.22	2.20, 3.03

CHAPTER **5**

Preparing the Results Section

The Results section should contain the summary of the findings, including the results of statistical analyses. The *Publication Manual* doesn't ask for much: only accurate, unbiased, complete, and insightful reporting of the data analysis (pp. 32–33). This section should be written in a form that is predictable. Report the statistical tests of your hypotheses in the order in which they were originally presented. Do not give in to the temptation to start with the finding you like best or end with the one that supports your favorite hypothesis. Don't leave out results that annoy you. Lead the reader through your analyses in the order that is most logical, not necessarily the one that is most exciting. Do not *discuss* which hypotheses were supported and which were not; those sentences belong in the Discussion section. This is not the place to concern yourself with variety of sentence construction. It is best to use the same sentence format for every result that involves the same type of statistic.

Results and Discussion can be combined into one section. This is often the case in published research when the two can be done relatively briefly. Many authors use this approach when reporting the results of more than one experiment in a single article. Each experiment contains a Results and Discussion section, and the article ends with a section entitled General Discussion. As a rule, students should have separate Results and Discussion sections unless directed otherwise by the instructor.

▲ **REMINDER BOX** ▼

Report results in the order that corresponds to the order of the hypotheses as presented in the introduction.

Statistics

In general, write for an audience that has substantial knowledge of statistical methods, but the audience will have to be persuaded if you do anything usual. You can do this by citing other authors who have demonstrated the usefulness and legitimacy of some new way of doing things.

Currently, researchers are at a crossroads in terms of null hypothesis testing (NHST). NHST is probably at the core of your own statistics classes and foundational in the training of your professors. However, in the sixth edition, the *Publication Manual* notes that "APA stresses that NHST is but a starting point and that additional reporting elements such as effect sizes, confidence intervals, and extensive description are needed to convey the most complete meaning of the results" (p. 33).

In general, you are asked to report per-cell sample sizes, observed cell means and standard deviations (or frequencies). For inferential statistical tests such as t tests, F tests, and chi-square tests, include the numerical value obtained for the statistic, degrees of freedom, and probability level (exact p value). Report effect size, if possible in original units as well as a standardized unit (such as eta squared, Cohen's d or regression coefficient). Reporting of confidence levels is strongly suggested. For F tests, also include the mean square of the error term (*MSE*). Indicate the direction of effect; for example, *Group A scored significantly higher than Group B* is better than *the scores of the two groups were significantly different*. You must report actual means and standard deviations (or some other measure of variability) whenever you report that means differed. These may be provided in a table.

▲ **REMINDER BOX** ▼

Whenever an effect is significant, report the direction of that effect.

Use brackets and the abbreviation CI for confidence intervals. Example: The smoking group had a 17% risk of experiencing rude glances, 95% CI [12.3, 21.0].

Students are usually required to report a bit more information than is included in journals. For example, after a *t*-test result, you must indicate whether it was one-tailed or two-tailed. Also, you will have to include statistical values for all of your results, even the nonsignificant ones. Please note that the word *insignificant* does not belong in your paper. That is not a technical term; it is an insult. If you mean that the result was not significant, you should use the word *nonsignificant*. No one will be insulted that way.

▲ REMINDER BOX ▼

Use *nonsignificant* rather than *insignificant* if an analysis does not yield an acceptable level of significance.

The *Publication Manual* advises that you report exact *p* values to two or three decimal places. Report *p* values less than .001 as *p* < .001. In tables, it may be clearer to use only the rounded values of < .05, < .01, and < .001. More on this later, in the section on tables. The main thing to remember in reporting probability is to use the *less than* symbol and the *equals* symbol appropriately. If the value comes from a statistical package, use the *equals* symbol (e.g., *p* = .023) and report two or three decimal places, whichever your statistical output provides. But note this exception: If the statistical package output indicates a probability level of .000, you should write *p* < .001. A *p* value cannot be zero, so .000 from a statistical package (like SPSS) indicates that the probability has been rounded off. The real probability might have been .0000071. If you drop the last zero in the value on your printout and replace it with a 1 and then claim that *p* < .001, you have made an accurate statement (.0000071 *is* less than .001).

There are only a few ways to phrase statistical reports. Collect some models now. Use only very recent journals for this exercise because the older journals might follow rules that are out of date.

Exercise 1

Copy sentences that contain *t*-test results. Note that "*t* test" is hyphenated when it is used as a compound adjective (as in *t*-test results) but not otherwise. Note also that statistical symbols are italicized.

1. Overall mean ratings of freshness did not differ as a function of age, $t(49) = .03$, *ns* ($M = 6.12$, $SD = 1.37$ for old and $M = 6.50$, $SD = 2.01$ for new).

2. There was a tendency for managers to rate themselves as braver than did their employees, $t(50) = 12.37$, $p = .072$.

3. Independent sample one-tailed t tests showed that dogs scored significantly higher than cats on both the first test battery, $t(29) = 22.42$, $p = .021$, and on the second test battery, $t(29) = 19.32$, $p = .032$, Cohen's $d = 1.84$.

4. _____

   _____

5. _____

   _____

Exercise 2

Copy sentences that contain chi-square results. Note that Greek letters are not italicized. Degrees of freedom and sample size are included in parentheses. Degrees of freedom are included for most other statistics as well, but sample sizes are not. You are also required to report cell frequencies, but these often appear on a table.

1. There was a significant relationship, $\chi^2 (1, N = 31) = 10.4$, $p = .01$, between type of bird (chicken or turkey) and whether the gravy was with giblets or without.

2. _____

   _____

3. _____

   _____

Analysis of variance results usually contain the abbreviation ANOVA. The rule for abbreviations is the same for the Results section as for the rest of the manuscript. Introduce the abbreviation in parentheses the first time you use the term, and then use only the abbreviation thereafter. If you do not use the term a second time in the manuscript, do not introduce the abbreviation at all. The abstract does not count as part of the manuscript for this rule.

▲ REMINDER BOX ▼

Introduce abbreviations in parentheses and use the abbreviations rather than the full term thereafter.

Usually, the *F* test is reported for the ANOVA. Students have varying degrees of familiarity with ANOVA results. Undergraduates are likely to have experience with one-way analyses and analyses using two independent variables. Therefore, these will be the focus here.

If you compared three or more means in a one-way analysis, report the results using the term *one-way analysis of variance*. Remember that a significant finding means that at least one mean was different. Because this lacks precision, authors usually do planned or post hoc tests on these means. Planned comparisons are reported as such. Post hoc tests are usually named (e.g., Tukey or Scheffe), and a significance level may be targeted prior to the calculation, depending on the statistical package you use. You are also expected to provide cell means, cell standard deviations, and an estimate of the pooled within-cell variance. These often appear on a table. Effect size is usually reported as η^2 (eta squared) with *F*-test results: $F(1, 115) = 623.16$, $MSE = 7.01$, $p < 0.1$, $\eta^2 = .83$. You can only be sure of finding effect sizes in the most recent journals.

Exercise 3

Copy sentences from Results sections that report one-way ANOVAs. If planned comparisons or post hoc tests were done, include those sentences.

1. We analyzed mood judgments using a one-way ANOVA. Participants in the elated condition rated themselves most elated, followed by participants in the neutral condition and those in the positively grim condition, $F(2,100) = 21.35$, $MSE = 7.95$, $p = .004$, $\eta^2 = .23$. See Table 1 for means and standard deviations.

2. _____

3. _____

_____

_____

_____

4. _____

_____

_____

_____

Analyses with two independent variables require the reporting of main effects and interactions. The safest way to report these is either with both main effects preceding the interaction or with the interaction first. Do not report one main effect, the interaction, and then the other main effect. As with *t* tests, if you say that a main effect was significant (e.g., "The main effect of color was significant"), take the opportunity to say right at that time what the direction of the effect was (e.g., "The main effect of color was significant, with the blue-pencil group scoring higher than the green, F . . ."].

Interactions generally leave you two choices for phrasing: (a) "The interaction between age and instructional condition was significant, F . . ." or (b) "The Age × Instructional Condition interaction was significant, F . . ." Capitalization rules are somewhat unexpected: main effects are lowercase, but interactions (when you are using the multiplication symbol) are capitalized.

Do not be concerned that you have several sentences in a row that are the same in structure. The reader will not be put off by this but rather will appreciate the clarity.

▲ REMINDER BOX ▼
Capitalize interaction terms but not main effects.

Exercise 4

Find sentences that report 2 × 2 ANOVA results. Copy what you find, including main effects and interactions.

1. We examined mean cooking times for experimental and control ovens using a 2 (gender) × 2 (condition) analysis of variance (ANOVA). Overall, men cooked more slowly than women, $F(1, 62) = 60.51$, $MSE = 27.74$, $p < .0001$, $\eta^2 = .34$. Cooking was on average 1.1 s slower in the control oven, $F(1, 62) = 40.32$, $MSE = 16.21$, $p = .003$, $\eta^2 = .21$. The Gender × Condition interaction was significant, $F(1, 62) = 29.11$, $MSE = 2.20$, $p = .031$, $\eta^2 = .45$.

2. A 2 (gender) × 2 (oven type) ANOVA was computed. The main effect for gender was significant, with men cooking more slowly than women, $F(1, 50) = 18.10$, $MSE = 3.21$, $p = .004$, $\eta^2 = .08$. The main effect for oven type was significant, $F(1, 50) = 21.44$, $MSE = 32.81$, $p = .002$, $\eta^2 = .32$, with faster times for the microwave than for the conventional oven. The Group × Oven Type interaction was not significant.

3. _____

_____

_____

_____

4. _____

_____

_____

_____

5. _____

_____

_____

_____

Correlation results require the correlation coefficient, r, and the p value. Reporting correlation results can be a preposition nightmare. These are acceptable statements of correlation:

X correlated significantly with Y.

X and Y were significantly correlated.

The correlation between X and Y was significant.

The correlation of X and Y was significant.

Correlations among X, Y, and Z were computed.

The correlation of X with Y was significant.

Exercise 5

Copy sentences that contain correlation results.

1. The correlation between swimming speed and hiking speed was not significant, $r = .17$.

2. The correlation between age and facial expressivity was not significant, $r = .06$. The correlation between shoe size and facial expressivity was significant ($r = .51$, $p = .003$).

3. _____

   _____

4. _____

   _____

5. _____

   _____

You must report means and standard deviations, but you do have some choice about where. They may be presented in a table, in the text, or in parentheses right after the statistic that compared them.

▲ REMINDER BOX ▼

When statistical analyses are used to compare means, provide all relevant means and standard deviations in the text or in a table, but not in both.

Even if you have decided to list means and standard deviations in the text as a way to avoid the difficulties of creating tables and figures, you are not off the hook yet. You face the decisions of where to put them and how to refer to them. You can put them after the statistic that indicates that they are significantly different from each other. If there are two means, use the word *respectively* to indicate order: "Mean scores for meat eaters and vegetarians were 6.10 (SD = 0.43) and 5.12 (SD = 0.23), respectively." Do not forget standard deviations. You can also squeeze this information into the sentence that reports a *t*-test result by using parentheses. You should use abbreviations for mean (M) and standard deviation (SD) when they are in parentheses: "Meat eaters (M = 6.10, SD = 0.43) scored significantly higher than vegetarians (M = 5.12, SD = 0.23), *t* . . ." Always indicate what the mean refers to (e.g., mean ratings, mean scores, mean number correct).

Exercise 6

Copy sentences from Results sections that contain information about means and standard deviations.

1. A post hoc test showed that race car drivers (M = 100.00 mph, SD = 10.13) and go-cart drivers (M = 101.30 mph, SD = 8.45) drove at significantly higher speeds than did bus drivers (M = 48.15, SD = 7.02).

2. Women had, on average, longer fingernails than men (women: M = 8.35 cm, SD = 0.83, men: M = 6.42 cm, SD = 0.65).

3. _____

_____

4. _____

_____

5. _____

_____

Manipulation Check

It is your responsibility to demonstrate that your manipulation actually manipulated your groups. So, for example, if you manipulated the instructions for a task, include some measure that indicates that participants attended to the instructions. If the materials differed by condition, make sure that participants noticed the part of the stimulus that you manipulated. If there was an intervention, make sure that the intervention was delivered appropriately. Results of this check on your method should be included in the Results section.

Data Displays: Tables and Figures

Tables typically contain expanded data not otherwise presented in sentence form elsewhere in the Results section. However, you may see word tables that, for example, show how conditions were organized or what stimuli were used. *Tables always have rows and columns.* A figure can be, for example, a flow chart, a photograph or drawing that illustrates the stimuli used in an experiment, or a graph. *Figures do not have rows and columns.* Here we will focus on only data tables and graphs. Tables are good for presenting data when you want to be precise. Graphs are better for illustrating patterns in your results.

Tables and graphs are used sparingly because presenting too many tables can be inconvenient for readers and expensive to publish. The *Publication Manual* suggests that some of this material might be better presented online in supplemental materials archives, particularly if the material is not essential to one's understanding of the text, but rather would augment it. You may come across this situation in your reading, but as a student it is most likely that your professor will instruct you to present certain findings in tabular or graphic fashion to give you practice.

General rules that apply to both tables and graphs are specified in the *Publication Manual* (p. 126): It is convenient for the reader to see items next to each other if you intend for the items to be compared. Labels should be close to the items to which they refer. The reader should not need a magnifying glass to read the text. Tables and graphs should be understandable without close reading of the text, so abbreviations should be obvious or they should be explained in a note. Make it attractive, but value clear communication over decoration. Although everything else in your paper must be double-spaced, you can use single spacing on tables if that enhances clarity.

Tables and figures should be numbered in the order in which they occur in the text. The first table that you mention is Table 1 and the first graph that you mention is Figure 1. Tables need titles, and graphs need captions. These are really different words for the same thing. They both give an indication of which variables they contain but should not completely duplicate the labels already in them. For example, *Mean Happiness Ratings for All Conditions* is better than *Mean Happiness Ratings and Standard Deviations for Fun Condition, Pain Condition, and Basketball Condition.* Graphs typically have an *x* axis and a *y* axis. A good caption often just states *Y as a Function of X* or *Happiness Ratings as a Function of Condition and Time of Day.*

Certain types of tables and graphs have been used so often that they have developed canonical forms. These function as templates and you should always look for such an existing format to present your data before inventing something of your own. You can find some of them in the *Publication Manual*, in printed journals, and in two helpful books by Nicol and Pexman: *Presenting your findings: A practical guide for creating tables* (1999) and *Displaying your findings: A practical guide for creating figures, posters, and presentations* (2003).

> **This article has some good examples of both tables and graphs**: Jimeno-Ingrum, D., Berdahl, J. L., & Lucero-Wagoner, B. (2009). Stereotypes of Latinos and Whites: Do they guide evaluations in diverse work groups? *Cultural Diversity and Ethnic Minority Psychology, 15,* 158–164.

Exercise 7

Find one table and one graph that you understand. Copy the table title and figure caption here:

Table title: _____

_____

Figure caption: _____

_____

Tables

Locate the table number in the upper left corner of the page and place the title, italicized, below it. Align columns carefully with plenty of space between columns. Note that APA-style tables have horizontal lines at the start of the table, separating each row of headers, and spanning the last row of data. There are no grid lines separating rows and columns of data. Use the tables feature of your word-processing program. When you have finished, make sure that you have removed from view all of the unnecessary gridlines and kept only the required ones.

Most often, results of significance tests (for example, ANOVA results) should be in the text. However, if there are a lot of means and standard deviations to report, then a table is convenient. Obviously, a table with only three numbers probably presents data that could more conveniently be provided in the text. Means tables should include standard deviations (these can be in parentheses following the means with a note to that effect below). Whenever possible, tables should include confidence intervals as well, using brackets (as in the text) or using columns for upper and lower limits. You will not find examples of confidence intervals very often before 2010, or even 2011, because it is a new requirement.

Now consider the words identifying the rows and columns. Every column needs a heading. You can use standard abbreviations and symbols here, for example *M* and %. Often, column headings are organized into several layers (two is usually enough). The bottom headings refer directly to the numbers below them. The one above is called a *column spanner*. It can be used to avoid repeating words that belong to more than one heading. So with a 2 × 2 design and several scale scores to report, you might stack one variable under the other. Here is a sample:

Table 1

Mean Scores by Grade Level and Condition

	First Grade		Second Grade	
Scale	Noise	Quiet	Noise	Quiet

Below this you would provide the columns of data, ending with another line spanning across. Under that line go any notes that are necessary to understand the table. If you need a general note, type the word *Note* in italics followed by a period flush left under the final line spanning the table. Then explain what you need to explain: for example, the meaning of unusual abbreviations or the fact that standard deviations are in parentheses. Follow it with a period even if it is not a full sentence. A probability note would come next, if appropriate, and it explains how you have indicated *p* values in the table. Use asterisks for this:

$*p < .05. **p < .01. ***p < .001.$

Use only the ones you need and be consistent with it across all the tables in your paper.

Exercise 8

Find two tables that display data you understand. Copy the titles of the tables and the headers.

1. Title: _____

_____

Column headers: _____

_____

2. Title: _____

_____

Column headers: _____

_____

If you do use a table, you must refer the reader to it by number and indicate what will be found there. This is a good time to think about verbs and sentence subjects again. If a table is to be the grammatical subject of a sentence, just what can it do? Do tables *contain* numbers? Do they *display* them? Perhaps. Alternatively, the contents of the table may be the grammatical subject, and then you must figure out what relationship the contents have to the table. Are numbers *on* a table? *In* a table?

Exercise 9

Find out now just what acts tables can legally perform. Copy sentences from Results sections that refer readers to tables.

1. Table 3 presents correlations . . .

2. Table 3 indicates frequencies . . .

3. Table 4 summarizes the results of the regression analysis.

4. Mean scores appear in Table 4.

5. _____

6. _____

7. _____

Graphs

Directly below the figure, type the word *Figure* in italics, then the figure number followed by a period. The figure caption follows that. It contains a short descriptive phrase like a title, but that may be followed by other information of the sort that might be found in a table note. Don't capitalize all major words as you would in a title. For example:

Figure 1. Mean relationship satisfaction as a function of degree completed. Relationship satisfaction was rated on a scale from 1 to 10. Error bars represent standard errors of the means. Asterisks indicate significant differences between conditions, $p < 0.5$.

Line graphs and bar graphs are very common in psychology journals. It is best to produce your graphs with a graphics program that allows a degree of customization. That way you will be able to follow a lot of very specific APA guidelines, a few of which are presented here. The independent variable is plotted on the x axis, and the dependent variable is plotted on the y axis. The y axis should be shorter than the x axis (the y axis is often about two-thirds the length of the x axis). Choose a scale that includes all the data without a lot of empty space. The axes must be labeled, and the unit of measure must be included in the label. Lines should be smooth and sharp, and the typeface should be simple and easy to read (e.g., Arial or Helvetica). Type size should be consistent throughout the figure, between 8 and 14 points. Use shadings to distinguish bars on a graph, making them maximally distinguishable, like black and white. Do not use color. Do not show gridlines.

For a line graph, differentiate lines by differentiating plot points. Use clear, open, and solid circles and triangles as plot points. Lines should all be solid rather than dashed or dotted. For a bar graph, use simple shading techniques to distinguish among sets of bars. White (no shading) and black are preferable to grays and stripes. If you need a third shade, use diagonal stripes. Do not use color for graphs.

Place a legend inside the graph area. Use it to explain the meanings of the shapes of the plot points or the shadings of the bars in the legend. Important words in the legend are capitalized.

When referring the reader to the graph of your results, you face the problem of subject and verb again. What can a figure legally do? What relationship do the contents of the figure bear to the figure itself?

Exercise 10

Copy sentences from Results sections that refer readers to figures.

1. Inspection of Figure 3 indicates . . .
2. As can be seen in Figure 2 . . .
3. Figure 1 illustrates . . .
4. _____
5. _____
6. _____

▲ REMINDER BOX ▼

Refer to all tables and figures at least once in the body of the paper.

General Placement of Tables and Figures

Every table and figure should be on its own page with the same page header (running head plus page number, see Chapter 9) as the rest of the text. They should be placed after the References section, first the tables and then the figures.

Useful Rules

1. Letter symbols (e.g., N, p) are italicized.
2. Greek letters are not underlined or italicized.
3. Letters that are abbreviations (e.g., M, SD) should be used only in parentheses. In the narrative, use the word (e.g., mean, standard deviation).
4. Use the symbol for percent (%) whenever it is preceded by a numeral (e.g., 3%).
5. Use spaces between symbols and within equations as if each term were a word (e.g., $p = .05$).
6. Use numerals for 10 and above; use words for nine and below.

Exceptions:
a. Never begin a sentence with a numeral. Look up spellings for numbers in the dictionary and pay attention to hyphen use. Try not to begin a sentence with a number.
b. Use numerals below 10 in an abstract.
c. Use numerals below 10 that immediately precede a unit of measurement (e.g., 5 ml)
d. Use numerals below 10 to represent times, dates, ages, scores, points on a scale, sums of money, and points on a graph (e.g., a 5-point scale or a 5-year-old child).

7. Use metric units unless the nonmetric is more familiar (e.g., 3 × 5 cards). In this case, put the metric equivalent in parentheses.

8. Use a zero before a decimal point when the value of a number is less than 1, unless it can never be more than 1 (e.g., levels of significance, proportions, correlation coefficients).

9. Rounding off: Use two decimal places when reporting inferential statistics. Use exact p values to two or three decimal places and use $< .001$ when that is the fact. For means, use two decimal places as long as relevant differences can be seen with two decimal places. Otherwise, try to rescale, for example, converting centimeters to millimeters.

10. Abbreviations for any measurement you are likely to need are listed in the *Publication Manual*. Note that most, but not all, abbreviations for units of measurement are neither capitalized nor followed by a period. Leave a space between the numeral and the abbreviated unit of measurement.

11. The plural of *analysis* is *analyses*.

12. *Between* is used for two things: Correlations were computed *between* two variables. *Among* is used for three or more: Correlations were computed *among* three variables.

13. Word your sentences so that statistical results are not in parentheses. Many statistical results contain parentheses of their own (containing degrees of freedom, for example). Set off these statistical results with commas instead.

14. Do not use mathematical symbols as if they were verbs in your sentences. For example, the following is *incorrect:* The number of boys = 17. You can use the word *equals* if you really must write a sentence that uses it. The word *was* is also useful here. Use the symbol for mathematical terms when those terms are inside parentheses.

15. Common fractions are expressed in words (e.g., one-half of the sample, three-fourths of the liquid), and others are expressed as numerals (e.g., 31.2 pastries).

Looking Back and Looking Ahead

I warned you that it would get picky. In this chapter, I hope you learned to take nothing for granted. APA style even has a rule for how much space to leave after an equal sign (one space). Because this chapter focused on how to present your findings, all of which are the result of statistical analyses, it emphasized how these mathematical terms are expressed in prose. It is certainly a pain in the neck to learn all of this for the first time, but it is very convenient in the long run that everything is so standardized. It means that your reading is much easier. You can now go to any Results section and be pretty sure of understanding the findings that cover statistics you have learned. They will always look the same, if not quite identical to how they looked on your statistics class assignments.

In general, you should include the test statistic, the degrees of freedom, the p value, the direction of effect, the effect size, and the power. Very often, you will also need means and standard deviations, and these are often presented in tables or graphs. As you write this section, be aware of the need to learn or look up rules about using parentheses, italics, uppercase letters, numerals versus number words, abbreviations, and symbols like the percent symbol.

The next chapter will cover the Discussion section. You can relax about the pitfalls of writing mathematical and statistical symbols, and you can allow yourself to think about why it all matters. Discussion section woes are more likely to be about how to stretch a few thoughts into a draft that seems long enough to pass muster. However, in the next chapter, you will find many suggestions for how to discuss your results, and you will be surprised at how much you really do have to say.

For more information:

Topic	Publication Manual	Concise Rules
Results section generally	2.07	—
What details to report	2.07, 4.44	4.14
References for statistics	4.42	4.12
Confidence intervals	4.10, 4.44	2.11, 4.14

(continued)

Topic	Publication Manual	Concise Rules
Probability—reporting of *p* value	2.07, 4.35	4.05
t -test hyphen	4.13 General Principle 3	2.14 General Principle 3
Statistical symbols italics	4.21, 4.45	3.01, 4.15
ANOVA: abbreviation	4.22, Table 4.5	3.03, Table 4.1
Capitalization: names of factors, variables, effects	4.20	2.21
Choosing text, table, or graph	4.41	4.11
Table numbers	5.05	5.05
Table titles	5.12	5.12
Table headings	5.13	5.13
Ruler lines and line spacing in tables	5.17	5.17
Table checklist	5.19	5.19
Table notes	5.16	5.16
Standards for figures	5.22, 5.25	5.22, 5.25
Figure captions	5.23	5.23
Figure legends	5.23	5.23
Figure checklist	5.30	5.30
Statistical symbols in text versus parentheses	4.45	4.15
Spacing for mathematical expression	4.46	4.16
Numerals versus number words	4.31 to 4.34	4.01 to 4.14
Metric system	4.39	4.09
Zero before decimal point	4.35	4.05
Rounding off	4.35	4.05
Abbreviations for measurements	4.27	3.08
Parentheses with statistics	4.09 to 4.10	2.10 to 2.11
Fractions	4.32	4.02

CHAPTER *6*

Preparing the Discussion Section

The *Discussion* section contains three types of material. The first can be called *inevitable*. It is inevitable that the results will be evaluated in terms of the research questions and/or hypotheses generated in the introduction. Each statistical analysis was done in an effort to answer one of these questions or test one of these hypotheses. The results of these analyses have been reported in the Results section. In the Discussion section, you must, inevitably, indicate which analyses lead to what answers, or you must indicate which analyses support or do not support which hypotheses. When hypotheses are supported, you will then, inevitably, refer to the theory or theories that generated those hypotheses. When hypotheses are not supported, you will inevitably admit it and look back to the method and/or the theory for enlightenment. It should be clear that the inevitable part could be written by anyone who really understood the introduction and results.

The second type of material found in the Discussion section is *creative,* and the creative part can be written only by you. This type of creativity characterizes the creative researcher, not the poet. You need to step back mentally from your findings and think about what else might be interesting about them. If hypotheses are supported, are there other explanations that a creative thinker might come up with besides the happy thought that your hypotheses are simply perfect? In the case of hypotheses that are not supported, what possible explanations exist? Would it be reasonable to make a minor adjustment in a hypothesis in light of a given result, or are there confounding factors in the method? Here we are talking not about technical problems that result from undergraduate foul-ups, but rather about real methodological issues that might interfere with the results of the most sophisticated laboratory crew. If your results are entirely unexpected (perhaps even in the wrong direction), you can bring in literature that you did not mention in the introduction to place these unexpected findings in a new context. Most of the literature you refer to in the inevitable part of the discussion should have been mentioned in the introduction, but there are exceptions in this creative part.

The third part is *confessional*.* Here you consider the limitations of your study. You must admit that this is not the ultimate answer to the pressing problem you defined in your introduction. You must explain what cautions are necessary in interpreting this finding.

The *Publication Manual* provides less guidance for the format of the Discussion section than students would like. And because it is more creative and freewheeling than the other sections, it is difficult for students to know when they have written enough. They sometimes resort to noting trivial shortcomings (e.g., not enough participants) and overbroad applications (e.g., this study should help teachers of students with learning disabilities). However, it is possible to overlay a format of three unofficial sections on most fairly short Discussions. I will call them first part, second part, and third part so that you can conceptualize them. But remember that these demarcations are used here as guideposts—they are *not* to be used as subheadings in your actual Discussion section.

First Part: Inevitable

The Discussion should begin with an assessment of the results of your main hypothesis. Usually, the entire hypothesis is restated in a sentence concerning its support or nonsupport. It is appropriate to remind yourself at this point that your experiment was designed to test a hypothesis, not a theory. A theory probably led to the hypothesis, and support of many such hypotheses lends support to the theory, but you

---

* I am indebted to Margaret Gatz for suggesting this term.

must first deal with the hypotheses in your discussion. Students sometimes forget that experiments do not *prove* or *confirm* hypotheses. The best way to convert the inferential statistics in your results into plain English for the discussion is with the word *support* or the phrase *fail to support.*

▲ REMINDER BOX ▼

Start your discussion by referring to the main hypothesis. Indicate which statistical result appears to support it or fails to support it.

Exercise 1

Select several Discussion sections and look at the first sentence or two of each. Copy examples of opening passages that state whether or not the main hypothesis was supported. When several hypotheses have been tested and several statistics have been reported, you may find that the author indicates which specific result or analysis is tied to a specific hypothesis. However, the Discussion section is not a place to restate the results, but rather to explain and interpret them.

> *Here is an article that contains information about the main hypothesis at the start of the Discussion section (or choose your own):* Niu, W., & Liu, D. (2009). Enhancing creativity: A comparison between effects of an indicative instruction "to be creative" and a more elaborate heuristic instruction on Chinese student creativity. *Psychology of Aesthetics, Creativity, and the Arts, 3,* 93–98.

1. As expected, participants provided with salty foods requested more water than did those provided with unsalted foods.

2. The experiment reported here provides strong support for the general contention that the sun rises in the East.

3. The present findings fail to support the hypothesis that exterminators reliably detect termite infestations better than do third graders.

4. _____

_____

5. _____

_____

6. _____

_____

Recall that some studies are designed not to test hypotheses that imply direction of effect but rather to answer questions, describe characteristics, assess relationships, and so on. When this is the case, the word *hypothesis* will be missing from the first sentence of the discussion, but there will be some reference to the purpose of the experiment as it relates to the statistical analyses.

Exercise 2

Copy the first sentence or two of Discussion sections that refer to major results in terms of research questions or purposes other than hypothesis testing. *Hint:* Check first for Introduction sections that end with research questions rather than hypotheses. Then copy the first sentence of those discussions.

> ***This article will work here (or find your own):*** Kobayashi, F., Schallert, D. L., & Ogren, H. A. (2003). Japanese and American folk vocabularies for emotions. *The Journal of Social Psychology, 143,* 451–478.

1. The central findings of the experiment are that . . .

2. The results of Experiment 1 showed that . . .

3. _____

4. _____

5. _____

Second Part: Creative

After the general statement that refers back to the hypotheses or purposes in the introduction, you might find it difficult to classify all of the types of comments that follow. Authors have more leeway in this section than in the others. Try to find just a few examples of each of the kinds of comments that can be included in this section.

Exercise 3

Look for statements of similarity between this work and that of previous researchers or other works by the same author.

1. Our results support Ripley's belief that the truth is stranger than fiction.
2. Consistent with previous research, this study revealed that . . .

3. _____

4. _____

Exercise 4

Look for statements that show differences between this work and that of previous researchers or other works by the same author.

1. Given the data from our experiments, it is clear that liberty is not preferable to death, as Patrick Henry proposed.
2. Unlike previous studies, ours showed that graduate student trainees are indeed able to control their outbursts.

3. _____

_____

4. _____

_____

Exercise 5

Look for comments that refer to theories or theoretical contexts referred to in the introduction.

> ***You can find it here:*** Valle, A., & Callanan, M. A. (2006). Similarity comparisons and relational analogies in parent-child conversations about science topics. *Merrill-Palmer Quarterly, 52,* 96–124.

1. These findings suggest a limit to the use of the theory of relativity in explaining the motion of the planets.

2. Consistent with a mediation model, this study showed that . . .

3. _____

_____

4. _____

_____

5. _____

_____

Exercise 6

Look for acknowledgment of alternative explanations for the findings—explanations other than the "truth" of the hypotheses or theories that appear to be supported.

> *Here is an example:* Sweeney, P. D., & McFarlin, D. B. (2005). Wage comparisons with similar and dissimilar others. *Journal of Occupational and Organizational Psychology, 78,* 113–131.

1. Another possible cause for the higher death rates among the younger skydivers in this study could be their refusal to use parachutes.

2. One explanation for this inconsistency is . . .

3. _____

4. _____

5. _____

You must acknowledge negative results. What can you do with results that fail to support your hypothesis? In light of these results, you might reconsider the theory. What would be the ramifications of adopting a weaker version of the theory or, more extreme, of abandoning the theory? Perhaps your failure to extend a previous finding sheds light on the population to which it can reasonably be extended.

Exercise 7

Copy a few references to and explanations of negative results.

> ***This article contains an example:*** Montague, M., & van Garderen, D. (2003). A cross-sectional study of mathematics achievement, estimation skills, and academic self-perception in students of varying ability. *Journal of Learning Disabilities, 36,* 437–449.

1. The test did not reliably distinguish first-year college students from third-year students in their ability to spell correctly. It is possible that, contrary to our hypothesis, college attendance does not develop this skill. Alternatively, it may be that some majors are more likely to attract good spellers than others.

2. _____

   _____

   _____

3. _____

   _____

   _____

   Remember to discuss *all* of your results. If you just did one statistical analysis, you are ready to go on to the third part. If you tested more than one hypothesis or question, you will return to the first part and cycle through the second part again before going on. Begin the next section after you have discussed all of your results individually.

▲ REMINDER BOX ▼

Be sure to discuss the results of each of the analyses reported in the Results section.

The *Publication Manual* instructs that you discuss the implications of the work. *Implications* are the logical consequences and the larger significance of the outcome. If hypotheses are supported, implications are inevitable and should flow directly from a well-written introduction. The logical consequence of a supported hypothesis is a supported theory. This is, in itself, the larger significance of the outcome. The introduction will have made plain why this is valuable information. Restate some of these reasons. If hypotheses are not supported, you must think creatively and speculate about practical and theoretical implications. Try to end the discussion with a paragraph that makes it plain why psychologists, even those from other specializations, should find your work important.

Exercise 8

Find some words and phrases in Discussion sections that signal implications.

1. The present findings open a new window to the investigation of . . .

2. . . . makes a contribution to an accumulating literature . . .

3. If clinicians want their clients to develop to their maximum potential, they might consider [doing what I did with the experimental group].

4. _____

5. _____

6. _____

A specific type of implication can point to a practical application. For example, the significance of the work is that it provides guidelines for how people in certain situations should act or should be treated. But not all research has immediate practical applications. Some research is "pure" and will lead to applications only after much intervening research. If nothing practical comes to mind, do not force the point.

▲ REMINDER BOX ▼

A relatively easy and concrete item for discussion for the new researcher is the practical application of the finding. Do this if it seems reasonable for the type of study under discussion.

Exercise 9

List examples of how practical applications are mentioned in Discussion sections.

You'll find some here: Powers, T. A., Koestner, R., & Gorin, A. A. (2008). Autonomy support from family and friends and weight loss in college women. *Families, Systems, & Health, 26,* 404–416.

1. Researchers and clinicians should be careful about . . .

2. . . . recommend that memory improvement programs should emphasize . . .

3. _____

4. _____

5. _____

The last part of a Discussion section often contains suggestions for future research. Remember that this kind of suggestion must come directly from the discussion that precedes it. Sometimes students, feeling the need to suggest some future research, suggest something completely arbitrary. Be careful about this. For example, following a discussion of results related to a reaction time test of color naming, it is not appropriate to suggest that future research be done on color-blind people or people who speak other languages. A sure sign that you are falling into the trap of suggesting irrelevant future research is a sentence that begins, "It would be interesting to see whether . . ." Suggest future research only if you can suggest what the next *logical* research question would be. Don't forget the verb lessons you learned in studying the Introduction section: If "future research" is to be the grammatical subject of the sentence, your verb choices are limited.

Exercise 10

Copy phrases that indicate how suggestions for future research are tied to the rest of the Discussion.

1. Future research should focus on identifying the magnitude of the individual parts of the bigger thing whose magnitude I just identified.

2. Continued exploration of the relationship between the two variables [I studied] is necessary to determine which of the competing explanations for [what I found] accounts for how this happens outside the lab.

3. A study is needed that traces [this thing I found] by comparing two groups over time.

4. _____

_____

5. _____

_____

Third Part: Confessional

There should be a discussion of limitations in the study. This should not be a big part of any Discussion section, however. After all, if the experiment were truly weak, you would not have undertaken it. You should imagine yourself trying to outfox potential critics of your study and acknowledge its shortcomings yourself. This has the effect of making the reader feel intelligent for having noticed something before you even mentioned it rather than feeling argumentative about your conclusions.

Are the results generalizable to only a portion of the people to whom this hypothesis is supposed to apply? Of course. Indicate exactly what the limits of generalizability are. It is always possible to question the degree to which laboratory results generalize outside of the lab, but is there anything about yours that points especially strongly in that direction? Have you found significant but small effects? Is that a problem? Have you used correlation results to indicate the possibility of causality? Now is the time to remind the reader that this type of conclusion must be made with caution. Is it possible that someone else might have operationalized a construct in a different way than you did? Admit it. However, feel free to defend your decisions in the same paragraph.

▲ REMINDER BOX ▼

You are obligated to note the limitations of your study, but do leave out the trivial ones and the ones that might apply to any study ever undertaken.

Exercise 11

Look through Discussion sections for indications of the limitations of experiments. List the types of limitations that you find. You will have no trouble finding articles for this exercise.

1. The cross-sectional design does not give direct evidence of change in the variable of interest.
2. The findings are not generalizable to some other group.
3. The self-report method provides only an indication of how people actually behave in . . .
4. _____

   _____
5. _____

   _____
6. _____

   _____

Exercise 12

List specific words and phrases that are used to present limitations.

1. One limitation of the study is . . .
2. It could be argued that . . .
3. One concern is that . . .
4. At least two caveats should be mentioned . . .
5. _____
6. _____
7. _____

Sometimes the confessional section is the last part of the discussion. It is better, however, to slip it in before the implications. That way, you end with a brag instead of an apology.

Verb Tense

Remember the conceptual difference between past tense and present tense as it relates to a discussion of your research. Your experiment is over; your results have been analyzed. Reference to what you and your participants did and what you found is always in the past tense. Statements about human behavior in general are in the present tense. The implications of your study should be discussed in the present tense. As a result of these directives, your Discussion section is likely to be primarily in the present tense: Results *support* the hypothesis; limitations of the study *are;* findings *contribute* to the literature; the results *suggest;* they *support* the findings of other researchers; performance on these measures *involves.*

▲ REMINDER BOX ▼

Use past tense to describe your results and present tense for statements about human behavior in general and the implications of your results.

Exercise 13

List subject–verb phrases found in the present tense in Discussion sections.

1. One explanation that may account for the results is that . . .

2. When both parents are present, teenagers may feel inhibited.

3. Although these experiments demonstrate that the sky is blue, additional questions await further research.

4. _____

5. _____

6. _____

Exercise 14

List subject–verb phrases found in the past tense in Discussion sections.

1. The results of Experiment 3 showed that . . .
2. The present study examined . . .
3. Our results were probably not due to bad weather.

4. _____

5. _____

6. _____

Looking Back and Looking Ahead

In this chapter, you have learned that a discussion has three components. The first points to the outcomes of your hypothesis tests. The second elaborates on these outcomes, by referencing others whose results were either similar or different, by stressing theories that gained (or did not gain) support from the current results, by offering alternative explanations, and by suggesting important implications for the findings. The third component is the acknowledgment of weaknesses (but there is no need to flagellate yourself). These components do not need to be kept separate but can often be effectively interwoven.

Now that the research report is written, it is necessary to write an abstract. This is a very short summary that is placed at the beginning of the paper. The format is required in the social sciences and the sciences, but some students may not have seen it in humanities courses. The next chapter will explain how psychologists compose their abstracts.

For more information:

Topic	Publication Manual	Concise Rules
Discussion in general	2.08	—
Verb tense	3.06, 3.18	1.06, 1.18

CHAPTER **7**

Preparing the Abstract

The abstract is the part the reader approaches first, but the writer approaches last. By the time you are ready to write your first abstract, you will already have read and used abstracts for at least some of the purposes for which they are intended. And understanding what readers need from an abstract is the best way to begin learning how to fulfill these needs in your abstract.

Here are some of the types of readers you will be addressing:

1. *Someone who needs an overview of an article he or she is definitely about to read.* This reader might be a student doing required reading, an expert who is determined to keep up with everything written in a certain narrow field, or someone who was so attracted by the title that nothing will stop the process. This type of reader needs an outline that will facilitate cognitive processing of the article. Technical writing does not depend on surprise endings, and technical reading is aided when outcomes are known in advance.

2. *Someone who is browsing through a journal looking for something interesting to read.* This reader might be someone who subscribes to the journal (probably an expert) or someone passing time in

a library (perhaps an expert in a related field or a student). This reader appreciates the fact that all abstracts follow a similar format so that quick comparisons of content can be made. This person wants to know how a certain article will advance his or her professional knowledge—will it be relevant because of its theoretical context, methodology, or outcomes?

3. *Someone who is searching an abstract-retrieval system (such as PsycINFO).* This reader might be a student looking for sources for a paper, a professor looking for relevant readings to assign, an author deciding which journals are most likely to publish articles like the one he or she is preparing, a researcher looking for data on a measure, or a graduate school applicant looking for all of the articles written by the faculty of a program he or she is considering. Sometimes the outcome of these searches is a list of articles the searcher intends to look at or read. At other times, it is a fact-checking mission and begins and ends with abstracts only. Sometimes it is a fishing expedition, and the searcher may or may not decide to look at entire articles.

How can all of these types of readers be served by the same brief summary? There are two parts to the answer. First, the contents are narrowly specified in the *Publication Manual.* Therefore, readers will always be able to predict that they will find certain types of facts in every abstract. Second, the style is designed so that it can stand alone and still be very informative.

Location and Length

Place the abstract on its own page right after the title page. The word Abstract should appear centered at the top in the same font as the text—neither bold nor italic. The abstract is one paragraph, but it is *not* indented.

Every scholarly journal contains instructions to authors. The *Publication Manual* indicates that the typical length of an abstract is 150 to 250 words. This is true for APA journals, but be aware that related fields have other conventions, even while using the APA style guidelines in all other matters. For example, counseling journals tend to require abstracts well under 100 words, and medical and biomedical journals may specify a length well over 250 words. Use guidance from your instructor if you are assigned to write an abstract.

```
▲ REMINDER BOX ▼
```
The length of an abstract is specified by the journal in its instructions
to authors. It is typically 150 to 250 words in psychology journals.

Contents

The abstract of a research report should contain key facts from each
section of the report. Try using about one sentence each with information from the Introduction, Results, and Discussion sections and up to
two sentences from the Method section. This general rule should keep
you within the required word limit while allowing for each of the types
of information specified in the *Publication Manual*.

From the introduction, extract the key element from the portion devoted to the purpose of the study and reduce it as much as you
can. This information is usually contained in the first sentence of the
abstract.

Exercise 1

Find the first sentence of abstracts that begin with a global statement of
purpose. Copy those sentence frames.

> *You will find a good example here:* Alexander, P. C. (2009).
> Childhood trauma, attachment, and abuse by multiple partners.
> *Psychological Trauma: Theory, Research, Practice, and Policy,*
> *1*, 78–88.

1. Aims were to determine _____ and identify related
variables.

2. The effectiveness of _____ on the _____ functioning
and mental health of _____ was examined.

3. To determine whether _____ and _____ with and
without _____ complaints differ in the nature of the activities they do in _____ circumstances, the authors developed
and evaluated the _____ scale.

4. _____

_____

5. _____

_____

    You must state facts about the participants that are particularly relevant to the study. Include at least number, age, and gender. If participants are not human, include genus and species.

Exercise 2

Copy statements from abstracts that provide facts about subjects or participants.

> *You will find a good example here:* Ko, K. J., Berg, C. A., Butner, J., Uchino, B. N., & Smith, T. W. (2007). Profiles of successful aging in middle-aged and older adult married couples. *Psychology and Aging, 22,* 705–718.

1. Fifty men and 52 women from a suburban population (age 26–64) . . .

2. The study included 100 women and their mothers who were living in multigenerational households that included a child under age 5.

3. _____

_____

4. _____

_____

5. _____

_____

    State the major elements of the method, including the apparatus, test names, and/or procedures. If a well-known test is the main element you need to mention, it may be included in the same sentence as the participant description. Alternatively, if the method is unusual, you might need to use two sentences. Try to mention items or features that might be used as keywords in someone's electronic search.

Exercise 3

Copy statements from abstracts that provide facts about methods.

1. Participants viewed pictures of insects and described their wing shapes.
2. . . . watched televised doctors and lawyers who endorsed various laundry products.

3. _____

_____

4. _____

_____

5. _____

_____

     State the major findings. Do this in English, not entirely in statistics, but do include effect sizes and confidence intervals and/or significance levels. You will not have space for secondary findings. Indicate only those that refer to the major purpose expressed in the abstract.

Exercise 4

Copy statements of research findings from abstracts. Use the most recent you can find. These details are absent from most journals before 2010.

1. Tree trimmers with low versus high trimming speed retired later (64.13 vs. 40.51 years, $p < .001$, $\eta^2 = .23$).

2. _____

_____

3. _____

_____

4. _____

_____

Finally, the abstract contains a statement (of the type found in the Discussion section) concerning the conclusions, implications, and/or applications of the study. Choose from the following types of statements: what was demonstrated, the consequences of what was demonstrated, or in what way the study should be appreciated and by whom.

Exercise 5

Look at the final sentences of some abstracts. Copy statements or sentence frames that seem to summarize the major points of the Discussion sections.

1. In addition to the better known _____, the [measure used in this study] is an important predictor of . . .

2. For [one type of participant] depression was predicted by [certain variables] and for [the other type] it was predicted by [other variables].

3. Findings extended prior research by demonstrating that . . .

4. _____

   _____

5. _____

   _____

6. _____

   _____

▲ REMINDER BOX ▼

Include the major purpose, result, and contribution of your study in the abstract.

Style

The best way to write your own abstract is to follow the preceding guidelines without concern for length in your first draft. When you have done that, you will probably find that you have gone over the word limit. The first thing you may do to shorten it is to make sure you have not repeated the title. Before attending to some of the stylistic elements that will help to shorten your abstract, go over it to make sure that it is accurate and self-contained. This editing session might even increase the length of your abstract, but consider why it is so important. Many people, as described earlier, will never read your entire article. For their sakes, your abstract must be able to stand alone and to report reliably what is in the paper.

▲ REMINDER BOX ▼

An abstract is accurate and self-contained. Some people will never read the rest of the article.

So reread your abstract, making sure that you have not included new information and that you have included the major purpose, result, and contribution of your study. If you have extended or replicated someone else's work, reference to that work must also be in the abstract (authors' last names and year of publication). That way, someone following up the work of a certain author will find yours in a keyword search. However, there is no references list associated with the abstract. The full reference information for studies referred to in your abstract will be at the end of your paper in the regular references section.

Use the active rather than the passive voice (This study investigated . . . The authors examined . . .). Use verbs rather than their noun equivalents (*examined* rather than *an examination of*, *analyzed* rather than *an analysis of*). Reread with an eye to how your sentences can be strengthened accordingly. For example, do not write, "Participants were asked for their opinions about . . ." Change to more active language: "Participants rated . . ."

▲ REMINDER BOX ▼

Use active rather than passive voice in the abstract.

Now reread again, making sure this time that the abstract can stand alone. Do not use unusual abbreviations. Define terms that a psychologist with a different specialty might not know. If you have given your treatment groups nicknames or abbreviations, do not use them in the abstract (unless you will refer to them twice in the abstract—then present abbreviations in parentheses the first time, as you would in the paper itself).

After you are sure you will not need to add anything else to your abstract and assuming that you are over the word limit, it is time to see what characters, words, or phrases you can delete. First apply this rule that is specific to abstracts: use numerals instead of words for numbers under 10 unless they begin a sentence. Although the 6th edition of the *Publication Manual* is silent about how to use abbreviations in the abstract, it is common practice to use abbreviations that are generally understood by psychologists even if you are using the terms only once (e.g., ANOVA and WAIS-III).

Next, look for phrases that are not dense with information and try to omit them. For example, omit "the results revealed that" and "the conclusions are that." If you have not done so already, omit phrases that repeat information provided by the title of the paper.

See whether sentences can be combined to save words. For example, perhaps you can include participant and procedure information in one sentence: "Undergraduate students (25 men and 25 women) rated five types of odors." You might be able to combine purpose and results by reordering and combining: "The hypothesis that _____ was supported in an experiment that assessed _____."

Do not be discouraged if you are still over the limit. Writing an abstract is a very difficult task. Deleting words and phrases that have been written with great effort is an emotional and intellectual strain. Consider trading abstracts with a partner if you still cannot find a place to delete words. It is often easier to slash phrases from someone else's work than from one's own.

When you finally determine that your abstract fulfills all of the criteria discussed so far, you have only one task left. Imagine all of the people who might search an abstract-retrieval database and be glad to find your abstract. What keywords would these people be likely to use in their search? Make sure that all of those words are actually in your abstract so that all of these potential searchers will find your work.

▲ REMINDER BOX ▼

Include all the words that someone doing a keyword search would be likely to need.

Looking Back and Looking Ahead

Remember the five "Cs": an abstract is correct, (self-) contained, concise, and coherent, and it covers all the bases. The specifics follow from those: use numbers, abbreviations, active voice. And make it short. Some journals and conference submissions even require 50-word abstracts.

In the next chapter, trivia (that you thought had been left behind with the Results section) will return to your world. The APA format for references must be followed down to the last comma and ampersand (&). Enjoy!

For more information:

Topic	Publication Manual	Concise Rules
Abstract contents, location, length, format	2.04	—
Numbers as numerals, not words	4.31	4.01
Verbs: Active voice, present tense	2.04	—

CHAPTER **8**

Preparing the References Section

Students often notice that APA style has a *References* section instead of a *Bibliography*. The difference is important. In your References section, you list the works you have referred to in your paper. A bibliography is usually more extensive than a references list and may contain material that you read but did not cite. Your references list should be in one-to-one correspondence with the sources you have mentioned in your paper. It should be accurate; readers might wish to consult some of your sources for their own edification. It should not contain anything you did not actually have in front of your eyes; secondary sources should be listed when appropriate, rather than primary sources that you did not read.

▲ REMINDER BOX ▼

Include in the references section only those sources that you cited in your paper and only those that you actually consulted.

If you read only one chapter of a book, you must list only that chapter. Usually, this occurs in the case of an edited book with chapters by various authors. Sometimes, however, you will consult part of a book written by a single author. In this case, the *Publication Manual* provides specific formats for indicating which chapter and/or pages you consulted.

There are so many types of material that may be consulted that it is not necessary (or rather, not possible) to familiarize yourself with all of them until you need them. In this chapter, you will learn about the three most common types of references that occur in student papers: journal articles, chapters in edited books, and authored books (the same person[s] wrote the whole book). If you have used any of the other types, consult the *Publication Manual* for details.

Word Processing Hints

- The References section begins on a new page. Type the word References centered at the top of the page in the same font as the text—neither bold nor italic. The rest of the manuscript (with the exception of the Abstract and the items that come after the references) is continuous; that is, no other section begins at the top of a new page unless it happens to fall that way.

- Double-space everything on these pages, both within and between references on the list.

- Each entry should begin with a *hanging indent.* That means the first word is at the left margin, and all other lines for that reference are indented one-half inch. Do not space-space-space your way through these indents. Format it with your word processor. In Microsoft Word you'll find the command in the Format Paragraph menu. Go to the box labeled *special* and choose *hanging.* Start the same way with Corel Word Perfect and when you get to the Format Paragraph menu, click on *hanging indent.* Many people find that it helps to prepare the References section in block form, with no indent at all. Just press *enter* for each new entry. When you are finished, you can select the whole section and format it as explained above.

- Never type authors' first or middle names. Use only their initials and leave a space between initials.

- Leave one space after all of the commas and periods within the References section.

Alphabetizing

Alphabetize according to the last name of the author who is listed first in each source. Keep the following in mind:

- Do not rearrange the order of authorship of any given article or chapter. If the article lists the authors as Smith, R. T., & Jones, A. L., do not list them as Jones, A. L., & Smith, R. T.

- Works by the same author or by the exact same group of authors are listed by year of publication, the earliest first. If that rule fails (because they are the same year), alphabetize by title, but don't count *The* or *A*. Then put lowercase letters immediately after the year, and refer to the work in your paper by the year and letter: Smith (2010a).

- If you have the same author listed first with different coauthors for different articles, arrange them alphabetically, according to the second author of each entry. List Smith, R. T., & Jones, A. L. before Smith, R. T., & Marks, B. J.

- If an author appears as a single author of one source and the first coauthor of another, list the single-author source first and then the one with the coauthor (following the principle that "nothing" goes before "something"). List Smith, R. T. before Smith, R. T., & Jones, A. L.

Exercise 1

From a References section, copy two listings by the same author for works published in different years.

_____

_____

_____

_____

_____

Now copy two listings in which publications by two or more authors are headed by the same author.

_____

_____

_____

_____

Journal Article Reference

Author(s). (Year). Article title. *Journal Title, volume number, page numbers*. doi:
   Here are the rules:

1. Authors, last name followed by initial(s).
   - Use the ampersand (&) before the last author.
   - Place a comma between author names.
   - Place the comma before the ampersand, even if there are only two authors in the list.

2. Year of publication.
   - Place it in parentheses.
   - Follow with a period.

3. Title of the article.
   - Capitalize only the first word in the title and the first word after a colon (even if these are only little words like *the*), when applicable.
   - Follow this with a period.

4. Title of the journal.
   - Capitalize each important word.
   - Italicize the title of the journal.
   - Follow this with a comma.

5. Volume number of the journal.
   - Italicize it.
   - Follow it with another comma.

6. Issue number.
   - Almost never include this. Do so only if each issue of the year starts with page 1. Usually, scholarly journals begin each *year* with page 1 and each *issue* with the page that follows the last one in the previous issue.

- If you should have to include this, place it in parentheses after the volume number.
- Do not italicize it.

7. Page numbers.
  - Include the full range (e.g., use 125–127 rather than 125–7 or 125–27).
  - Do not italicize the page numbers.
  - Finish up with a period.

8. Digital object identifier (DOI)
  - You may have noticed that retrieving from the Internet is unreliable. Here today, gone tomorrow. The DOI will never do you wrong. If the article is available electronically, the DOI will always be attached to that article, no matter what database you find it in.
  - The DOI is an alphanumeric string located on the first page, near the copyright information.
  - When you have a DOI, type *doi:* after the final period that comes after the page number. Then type it carefully or cut and paste it. Don't put any punctuation after it.

Journal article examples:

- One author:
  Rogers, M. (2010). My sweater has a zipper. *Children's Television Review, 12,* 120–122. doi:10.1037/a0013349

- With two authors, use an ampersand and comma between them:
  Rogers, M., & Kermit, F. (2009). Not all sweaters have zippers. *Children's Television Review, 14,* 12–30. doi:10.1037/a0013349

- With three authors:
  Rogers, M., McDonald, R., & Kermit, F. (2012). Not all creatures wear sweaters. *Children's Television Review, 17,* 124–130. doi:10.1037/a0013349

- All of those rules work for one to seven authors. With more than seven authors there is trouble. Name the first six, then three ellipses (. . .), then the last author:
  Rogers, M., McDonald, R., Kermit, F., Bird, B., Mouse, M., Brown, C., . . . Szuchman, L. (2000). What a pain in the neck. *Journal of Too Many Rules, 7,* 413–414.

Exercise 2

Find a journal article and cite the reference as it would appear on a references list.

_____

_____

_____

Chapter in an Edited Book

Chapter author(s). (Year). Chapter title. In Book Author(s) (Ed[s].), *Book title* **(page numbers of chapter). Place of publication: Publishing company. (Use DOI if available.)**

Here are the rules:

1. Chapter author(s)' last name(s) followed by initials.
   - Same rules as for journal article.
2. Year of publication.
   - Same rules as for journal article.
3. Title of the chapter.
   - Same rules as for journal article.
4. The word *In*.
5. Editor(s)' name(s).
   - Initial(s) then last name—not last name first.
   - Separated by commas and ampersand as for authors, but no comma for only two authors.
6. (Ed.) or (Eds.).
   - Follow with a comma.
7. Title of the book.
   - Italicize it.
   - Capitalize only the first word in the title and the first word after a colon, when applicable.
8. Page numbers of chapter.
   - Use the form pp. xx–xx.
   - In parentheses.
   - Follow with a period.

9. Place of publication.
   - ■ City and state or city and country.
   - ■ Use postal abbreviations for state.
   - ■ Follow with a colon.

10. Publishing company.
   - ■ Can be brief; for example, omit *Co., Inc., Publishers.*
   - ■ If same as author (e.g., American Psychiatric Association), use the word *Author* in place of publisher's name.
   - ■ End with a period.

Chapter in an edited book example:

Smith, T. J., & Jones, R. N. (1971). Very interesting stuff: Relationship between grades and dental cavities. In J. Lennon, & P. McCartney (Eds.), *A big book of interesting stuff* (pp. 22–125). London, England: British Books.

Exercise 3

Copy one listing from a References section for a chapter in an edited book.

_____

_____

_____

An Authored Book

Author(s). (year). *Title*. City: Publisher. (Continue to use DOI if available.)
     This is a book written entirely by the same author(s), rather than with chapters contributed by various people.

Authored book example:

Smart, I. M. (1995). *Fun with psychology.* Green Hill, IL: Green Publishing.

Exercise 4

Write the listing for this book as it would appear in a References section.

Electronic References

In most cases, you will be able to follow the rules above: author, date, title, and so on. Include as much of this as possible and then add the electronic retrieval information. If you have a DOI, that is all the retrieval information you need. Otherwise, you'll need the URL. If you are pretty sure that the source will not change, you don't need the retrieval date. If it is the type of source that does change, like a Wiki, you'll need the retrieval date as well. I hope you will not use those sources.

Here is an example:

Simpson, B. (1999). *Cartooning and psychology.* Hollywood, CA: American Psychological Association. Retrieved from http://www.apa.org/journals/simpson.html

The best case is the electronic version of a print journal article that you download as a PDF file. All the usual information will be there. You are looking at an exact copy of a journal article. Usually it is also available in print, so you have finished the job. If the journal is not available in print and you used a PDF, and if there is *no* DOI, then you have to find the home page URL of the journal. Don't use the database that you found it on. Search the web to find the homepage of the actual publisher.

For example, say I need to know about early maternal separation and how it relates to symptoms of activity-based anorexia in male and female rats. This 2009 article by Hancock and Grant is in the *Journal of Experimental Psychology: Animal Behavior Processes.* I can do so at no cost from my university library's online journal collection. The university subscribes to a database called PsycARTICLES and I can link to the article from there. There is a DOI: 10.1037/a0014736. So I just read the PDF version, reference it the normal way, and include the DOI. If there were no DOI, I would have to notice that it is published by APA, and I would go to APA.org and start surfing till I find the abstract at http://psycnet.apa.org/index.cfm?fa=buy.optionToBuy&id=2009-10283-008&CFID=23379563&CFTOKEN=78239404 and the opportunity to purchase the article for $11.95. Instead of providing the DOI, I would do this at the end (no period after the URL).

> Retrieved from http://psycnet.apa.org/index.cfm?fa=buy .optionToBuy&id=2009-10283-008&CFID=23379563& CFTOKEN=78239404

Try not to break a URL at the end of a line, but if you must, do so before a punctuation mark. Do not put a period at the end—that may cause the reader to include it in the retrieval and then it won't work.

Worst case: You want to cite a website that has no author, no year, no page numbers. See http://www.apastyle.org/learn/faqs/cite-website-material.aspx and hope for the best. Notice that what I just did is also the way to cite an entire website rather than an article: give the address in the text and put no entry in the references list.

Capitalization rules for URLs are as follows: Everything up to and including the host name (www.apastyle.org in the preceding example) is in lowercase. The rest must match exactly what you found on the web.

Exercise 5

Go to http://www.apa.org and search for a document you like. Cite it here:

_____

_____

References in the Body of the Manuscript

In the text, your citation would look like either of these:

> Smith and Jones (2010) found . . .
> The findings on altruism (Smith & Jones, 2010) . . .

As was noted in Chapter 2, the latter is usually preferred. The authors' names are typically not relevant to the point you are making, and if they are not directly relevant, then they are parenthetical.

When you are quoting from a source, use double quotation marks. Single quotation marks are only used when the author you are quoting is quoting someone else. In that case, the source contains double quotation marks, and these become single quotation marks in your manuscript. Final punctuation goes inside the quotation marks. When your quotation contains 40 or more words, use block form. That means that instead of using quotation marks, place the entire quotation in indented form. Indent one-half inch from the left margin (in line with the start of paragraphs) and keep every line of the quotation indented just the same amount. Do not change the right margin; use the same right margin as in the rest of your manuscript. Double space as usual.

You will have to cite the page number of the source for direct quotations. Do so after the closing quotation mark and before the period:

Freud (1950) reported, "Blah blah blah" (p. 23).

If you want Freud's name in parentheses, do it like this:

"Blah blah blah" (Freud, 1950, p. 23).

When this occurs after a block quote, it comes after the final punctuation:

Mary had a little lamb whose fleece was white as snow. Everywhere that Mary went, the lamb was sure to go. He followed her to school one day, which was against the rule. It made the children laugh and play to see a lamb at school. (p. 23)

Please recall the rule you read in Chapter 2: long quotations and frequent short quotations do not belong in a psychology paper.

Page references for online sources that are not paginated can be challenging. If paragraphs are numbered, use that number (e.g., para. 3). If they are not, use headings as locators (e.g., Explicit Communication section).

Here are some final quirks for referencing in the body of your paper:

- Use the ampersand in parentheses and the word *and* in the text.

  It was a nice day (Weatherson & Sunshine, 2008).

  Weatherson and Sunshine (2008) found daytime temperatures to be variable.

- Use commas only for three or more authors even though you use a comma for only two authors in the References section.

  Weatherson, J. P., & Sunshine, I. (2008). Sure has been nice weather lately: Extra good news. *Journal of Weather, 7,* 12–30.

  Many people go fishing when the weather is fine (Weatherson & Sunshine, 2008).

  Some disagree with that view (Sleet, Hail, Snow, & Rain, 2009).

- When the work has two authors, always use both names (Michael & Jordan, 1987). When it has more than two and fewer than six authors, name them all the first time you cite them (Reebok, Nike, Keds, & Converse, 1988). In future references to this work, name only the first and use *et al.* instead of the rest of the names on the list (Reebok et al., 1988). When the work has six or more authors, use *et al.* after the first author's name even the first time you cite them.

- If you are referring to more than one article inside the same parentheses, use a comma to separate two items by the same author(s) and a semicolon to separate between authors. List them in the same order as that in which they would appear in the References section. Here is an example: This hypothesis has received robust support (Ames, 1991, 2006; Roberts & Emerson, 1993; Simmons et al., 1990).

Referencing the DSM

What a nuisance! This is a book that psychologists reference all the time, and yet a very slippery bunch of rules apply. First of all, be assured that the APA feels your pain. All of the rules for this situation are at a website designed to teach you only about this one reference: http://supp.apa.org/style/pubman-ch07.02.pdf—and watch out because a revision of that book is on the way.

Meanwhile, at the time of this writing, you are citing the *Diagnostic and statistical manual of mental disorders* (4th ed., text rev.; *DSM-IV-TR*, American Psychiatric Association, 2000). There, I did it! Follow my lead. The next time you mention it in your paper, you just call it *DSM-IV-TR* (2000). There is an online edition as well, and if you use it you should also provide the DOI. In the References section it looks like this:

American Psychiatric Association. (2000). *Diagnostic and statistical manual of mental disorders* (4th ed., text rev.). Washington, DC: Author.

Looking Back and Looking Ahead

APA referencing style probably turned out to be less complicated than you might have thought, but as they say, the devil is in the details. You must follow the format exactly. The most striking difference between this referencing style and some others is that it contains only the works cited (although it does not have that name). Be sure to check that you have listed all the authors you have cited and that you have cited all the ones you have listed. Double-check the spelling of authors' names and work to make the references very accurate. Then work to make them conform to the style: authors' last names and initials, capitalization of only first word in article titles, commas in the right places, ampersands (&) as needed, italics for journal and book titles. Most important, look up the rules when you are not sure.

In the next chapter, you will learn how the first page of your manuscript should look and how to work with the settings on your word processor to conform to the final set of details.

For more information:

Topic	Publication Manual	Concise Rules
Accurate and complete reference list	6.22	7.23
Spaces after periods	4.01	2.01
Reference citations in text	6.11–6.31	7.12–7.22
Hanging indent	2.11	—
Alphabetizing	6.25	7.26
Author and editor information	6.27	7.28
Publication date	6.28	7.29
Title	6.29	7.30
Journal information	6.30	7.31
Book publisher information	6.31	7.31
Publishers' locations/postal abbreviations	6.30	7.31
Examples: periodicals	7.01	8.01
Examples: books and book chapters	7.02	8.02
Electronic sources	6.31–6.32 http://www.apastyle.org/learn/faqs/cite-website-material.aspx	7.32–7.33
Citing an entire website	http://www.apastyle.org/learn/faqs/cite-website.aspx	
Capitalization rules for URLs	6.31	7.32
Referencing *DSM*	http://supp.apa.org/style/pubman-ch07.02.pdf	

CHAPTER 9

Preparing a Title Page and Formatting Your Manuscript

Many people write with a working title in their minds but later find that the finished product is actually an imperfect match for the original title. Students working on laboratory assignments generally work from the title of the lab as listed in the syllabus, but that is often inappropriate for the actual research report. Therefore, it is common for both professionals and students to compose the final title after the manuscript is written.

Like any title page, the one for your APA-style manuscript contains the title of your paper, your name, and other identifying data. In addition, it contains information unique to APA style that is intended for the convenience of the editor and printer of the journal to which the article may be submitted: the manuscript page header and the running head.

Writing a Title

The *Publication Manual* directs that titles *should*

1. Be 12 words or fewer
2. Make sense standing alone

3. Name the important variables or theoretical issues

4. Identify the relationships among variables

A title *should not*

1. Contain abbreviations

2. Waste words (like *A Study of*)

It is no wonder that students need practice in writing titles that conform to all of these requirements. Often after accounting for variables and being sure to make sense, authors find themselves with very long first-try titles. Nevertheless, that is a good way to begin.

Write everything you think you need without worrying about length. At this point, it helps to think of the problem as a word puzzle, and very often word puzzles can be fun. First, get rid of anything unnecessary, such as "A Study of" or "An Investigation of." The title "An Investigation of the Relationship Between Hat Size and Performance in Undergraduate Research Methods Classes" would benefit from that kind of cleanup.

Now you might find yourself with a title that starts with the words "The Effect of" or "The Relationship Between." This is informative and does not break any rules, but it is not ideal. First, it is likely that you can save words if you find another way to convey this idea. Second, it is wise to begin with a word of specific importance to your study because when researchers glance through a list of titles in order to decide what to read, their attention is captured best by the first word. Choose your first word or phrase so that it applies uniquely to your own study. After all, every title of an experimental study could begin with "The Effect of." "Hat Size Effects on Performance in an Undergraduate Research Methods Class" conveys this uniqueness in the first words.

▲ REMINDER BOX ▼
Create titles that begin with important variables.

Exercise 1

It is worthwhile to look at some creative approaches to this "effect of" problem and work backward. Copy some titles that start with key words.

1. "Gender Influences on Face Recognition Errors." This works better than "Effect of Gender on Face Recognition."

2. "Manners and Monkeys: The Effect of Social Reinforcement in Teaching Primates to Use Forks." Sometimes authors put a catchy phrase up front and follow with "effect of."

3. "Do Mice Dream? The Relationship Between Rapid Eye Movements and Smiling in Sleeping Mice." Sometimes authors start with the research question and then move on to the variables.

4. _____

   _____

5. _____

   _____

6. _____

   _____

In scanning titles for Exercise 1, you undoubtedly noticed many that began with "The Effect of." You also saw some alternatives, and three probably stand out: the question title, the colon title, and the "and" title. The question title ("Do Mice Dream?") works because it is attention grabbing. The colon title works because it allows important variables ("Manners and Monkeys") to be named before the word *effect or relationship* is used, but these words can still be used for clarity. The "and" title names the variables, uses *and* between them, and requires that the reader infer which is the dependent and which is the independent variable. If you use an "and" title, be sure that there is little likelihood that a reader could make the wrong inference. ("Monkeys and Manners" is just as informative as "Manners and Monkeys.")

The Parts of the Title Page

Now that your title is written, you have only to follow some rules about getting it on a title page.

1. Type the title centered horizontally and in the upper half of the page. Capitalize each word, not the whole title. Use a font that matches

the one used in the body of the paper, and do not use bold type. If you use two lines because your title cannot fit on one line, double-space between them and break the title at a meaningful point, not whenever the line is full. "Gender Influences on the" is not a good first line for a two-line title.

2. Center your name one double space below the title. Decide today what your professional name will be. Most people use a first name and middle initial. But some people have names that are more complex than others, with two middle names or a hyphenated last name. Decide how it should look, but do not stray far from the first name–middle initial–last name approach. You might change your name between your first publication and your last, but you should not change your professional name if you want people to know who you are. Again, use uppercase and lowercase letters, nothing fancy. Do not use the word *by*.

3. Center the name of your institution one double space below your name.

4. Your instructor might want additional information, such as course number and date. If you have no specific instructions, just stop with name and institutional affiliation.

5. Decide on a running head of 50 characters (letters, spaces, and punctuation all count). The running head is a short version of your title that makes sense. If your title itself contains fewer than 50 characters, just use the title. The running head is what would be used as the page header in the actual printed journal and what helps readers to find their place or remember what they are reading. This running head is placed on all your pages flush left near the top and is identified as the running head on the title page. Here is an example:

Running head: TABLE MANNERS FOR PRIMATES

6. Create a manuscript page header. Use the layout menu (within the page set-up menu) to select a header style that has a different header for the first page. On the title page, the header contains the running head (along with the words *Running head* just as it looks in #5 above flush left, and a page number flush right. Make sure the font matches the rest of your paper (Times New Roman 12-point). This is what your header looks like for the title page.

Running head: TABLE MANNERS FOR PRIMATES   1

The rest of the pages do not contain the words *running head*. They look like this:

TABLE MANNERS FOR PRIMATES 2

▲ REMINDER BOX ▼

The running head of 50 characters or less makes sense and summarizes the title. It appears on every page, on the upper left.

Exercise 2

Copy some running heads (look in the upper margins of journal articles) and the titles of the articles to which they refer.

1. _____

2. _____

3. _____

Formatting

By the time you are preparing your title page, you are probably just about finished with your paper. Make sure you follow all of the general formatting rules for your paper:

1. Use Times New Roman 12-point font. You may use Arial or Helvetica in preparing graphs.

2. If you use special characters (e.g., Greek letters or multiplication signs for interactions), use the ones in your word processor ("insert symbol"). Don't just make it up (like using X instead of the symbol for chi, χ).

3. Start a new page after the abstract, for the references, and for each table and figure. Do not start any other sections with a new page.

4. Double-space everything. The only exception is that you may use single spacing or 1.5 spacing in tables.

5. Use at least a 1-inch margin on all sides. Your word processor's default setting should work fine for this.

6. Do not allow your word processor to right-justify your lines. The right margin should be "ragged." You might have to adjust your software's default settings to accomplish this. Look for an "alignment" command and choose "left." That way, you will get a straight left margin and a rough one on the right.

7. Do not allow your word processor to hyphenate at the ends of lines. This will probably also mean fiddling with default settings. Try finding "line and page breaks" somewhere in the paragraph or document formatting menu. Any hyphen that appears at the end of the line should be a "hard hyphen," one that belongs there whether it is the end of a line or not.

8. Use the tab function to set your paragraphs to indent one-half inch. But don't indent the abstract, certain headings that should be centered or flush left, figure captions, or items on your reference list (those should have a hanging indent).

9. The order of pages is

Title page

Abstract

Body of the paper

References

Tables

Figures

Appendixes

10. Use one space after commas, colons, some periods except
- No space within abbreviations (e.g., U.S., i.e.)
- Two spaces at the end of a sentence

11. Use your spelling-checker wisely. It can help you to spell words correctly if the word you have typed does not exist. It will not help you if you type *there* instead of *their.* Use your spelling-checker, and then use your brain.

▲ REMINDER BOX ▼

Do not begin the Method, Results, or Discussion section on a new page. Double-space throughout. The right margin should not be justified. Do not hyphenate at the ends of lines except when a hyphen is required as part of the spelling of that word.

Looking Back and Looking Ahead

In this chapter, you have noticed how difficult it is to create a title that is just right: it is concise, it differentiates your study from others with similar variables, it creates anticipation, and it identifies the important variables and relationships. You also learned that the title appears on a title page with five distinct elements: the title, your name, your affiliation, a running head, and a page number. Presenting a paper with this title page to a journal editor or an instructor is a way of saying that you are in the club, that you know the rules of writing of your profession. The reader will be more likely to approach your work with a positive, optimistic attitude.

You are now also aware of the other formatting rules for APA papers: the margins, the common font types, the spacing. Pay attention to the need to turn off automatic end-of-line hyphenation and to eliminate the justification of the right margin. These are other simple ways to look smart.

Now you have had practice with all the parts of your manuscript. The next chapter contains a selective grammar review, hitting the common mistakes of students and pet peeves of professors.

For more information:

Topic	Publication Manual	Concise Rules
Choosing a title	2.01	—
Author's name and affiliation	2.02	—
Elements of Title page	8.03	—
Running head	8.03	—
Font	8.03	—
Double-spacing	8.03	—
Margins	8.03	—
Justification, hyphen	8.03	—
Order of sections/parts	8.03	—
Page numbers and headers	8.03	—
Paragraphs and indentation	8.03	—
Spacing after punctuation	4.01, 4.40	2.01, 4.10

CHAPTER *10*

Grooming Tips for Psychology Papers

You would probably never think of getting ready to go to class without checking your hair. If you eat onions before class, you probably grab a breath mint. You would never leave the table without making sure there is no food on your face. You do not want people to think you are careless with your appearance, and you certainly do not want them to think you are messy or smelly. You want to make a good impression. In the same vein, why would anyone think that a good impression could be made by turning in papers with careless mistakes, messy grammar, and punctuation that offends?

Some people have a flair for prescriptive rules of grammar and punctuation. They seem to be born knowing how to avoid run-on sentences, for example. Others need to spend time learning these things, and some of these people get to college with a few gaps in their understanding.

This chapter contains a review of some rules of punctuation and grammar to which most college students have already been exposed. I have selected only a few rules because a psychology class is not the place to learn everything there is to know about grammar and punctuation. I have selected these particular ones because psychology papers seem to call for them quite often and, in my experience, psychology professors complain that many papers they grade contain errors based on the failure to apply these rules. For each of these rules, I have provided at least one example of proper usage in psychology journals. You will find others in doing the exercises.

Parallel Construction

Whenever elements of a sentence have the same function, their form has to be parallel. This simple rule must not be so simple, because so many students just cannot seem to get it right. Let's break it down. What elements of a sentence can have the same function?

Items in a Series

"The participants were women, over 21, and had red hair." The items in this series should all be nouns, all be adjectival phrases, or all be verb phrases, not all three.

Consider these examples.

"Participants were red-headed women over age 21." (This sentence no longer contains a series.)

"Participants were female, aged 21 or over, and redheaded." (This sentence contains a series of adjectives.)

Exercise 1

Find examples of parallelism in series. Underline the parallel words.

This article contains an example in the first sentence: McCullough, M. E., & Willoughby, B. L. (2009). Religion, self-regulation, and self-control: Associations, explanations, and implications. *Psychological Bulletin, 135,* 69–93.

In the same issue of the same journal, this article contains an example in the first paragraph: Courtney, K. E., & Polich, J. (2009). Binge drinking in young adults: Data, definitions, and determinants. *Psychological Bulletin, 13,* 142–156.

1. These included eating plums, preparing simple meals with plums, researching plums, selling plums, buying plums, and growing high-quality plums.

2. Low self-esteem is characterized by paranoia concerning bad hair, obsession with ring around the collar, and unwillingness to engage in violent confrontations.

3. _____

_____

4. _____

_____

Verb Forms

Verb forms must be parallel when they are joined in a series or by any kind of connecting word. There is an *error* in this sentence: "Participants were left alone and were being watched through a two-way mirror." *Were left alone* is not parallel to *were being watched.*

Correct it this way: "Participants were left alone and were watched . . ."

Here are some other examples.

"Dogs are more influential than cats, thereby occupying more leadership positions." *Are* is the third person plural present tense form of the verb; it is not parallel to *-ing*, which is a continuous or present progressive tense. Correct the sentence this way: "Dogs are more influential than cats, and therefore they occupy more leadership positions." *Occupy* is a third person plural present form. "Participants were asked to read, and they evaluated the stories." Both verbs should be passive or both should be active: "Participants were asked to read and evaluate the stories."

Exercise 2

Find examples of parallel verb forms with conjunctions.

1. Participants completed a questionnaire for the first 5 minutes, banged their heads on a wall for the next 5 minutes, and completed a second questionnaire in the final 5 minutes.

2. The psychology majors were praised and were given candy by the dean.

3. _____

_____

4. _____

_____

Half-Empty Comparisons

More likely than what? Older than whom? This type of question will keep you from writing sentences that can be ambiguous. If you are using the comparative form of an adjective (the *-er* form, such as *older, faster, or better*), be sure that the reader knows which two items are being compared. In conversation, this is usually not a problem. If you say, "It's more likely to rain today," your listener probably knows whether you mean more likely to rain than to snow or more likely to rain today than to rain tomorrow. Sometimes when you are writing, however, it is hard to remember that your reader is not as well informed about your context or your motives as a listener might be in conversation. So when you write that the experimental group performed better on the posttest, for example, your reader does not know whether that means better than on the pretest or better than the control group performed on the posttest. It is perfectly acceptable to write, "The experimental group performed better on the posttest than the control group did" or "The experimental group performed better on the posttest than on the pretest." On one of your drafts, read through just looking for comparatives and make sure they are unambiguous.

Another potential problem with comparisons is the failure to make the second part completely clear. This violation results in a sentence like this: "Participants rated the soda in the paper cups higher than the plastic." Did they like the soda better than the plastic?

Exercise 3

Find sentences that contain comparisons.

> *This article contains examples:* Lippa, R. A. (2003). Handedness, sexual orientation, and gender-related personality traits in men and women. *Archives of Sexual Behavior, 32,* 103–114.

1. Participants associated more positive emotions with the photographs of the house than with those of the elephant.

2. _____

_____

3. _____

_____

Agreement

Between Subject and Verb

Subject–verb agreement is typically a problem only when a number of words intervene between the subject and the verb. When that happens, there is a tendency to allow the verb to agree in number with whatever noun is nearby and seems to be the main topic of the sentence, even though that noun is not strictly the grammatical subject of the verb.

Exercise 4

Find a long sentence that really has only one subject and one verb. Underline the subject and the verb.

> ***Here is an example (sixth paragraph, fourth sentence):*** Trentham, S., & Larwood, L. (2001). Power and gender influences on responsibility attributions: The case of disagreements in relationships. *The Journal of Social Psychology, 141,* 730–751.

1. The goal of all but a few (and those few were the only naturalistic experiments ever conducted on communication between humans and mole rats) of Smith's studies was unfathomable.

2. The objectives of the study, albeit obscure and perhaps not amenable to unbiased interpretation by all but a few highly educated psychology students, as was common similarly in the research of Casteneda, were altruistic.

3. The unrealistic nature of the participants' responses to the frightening scenarios was surprising.

4. _____

_____

_____

Between Noun and Pronoun

Students come to college knowing that pronouns must agree in number with the nouns to which they refer. However, in writing psychology papers, students often fail to achieve perfect agreement between nouns and pronouns. The problem is most frequent with the possessive *their.* One cause is the effort to use the nonsexist phrase *he or she* as the subject of the sentence and then later referring to *their* left hand, for example. Remember also that *or* signifies a singular, not a plural, situation. The same goes for *each* (each person *cannot* use *their* pencil). This type of error is so common that you should give your paper a read-through just to check every *their* against its referent. The solution will usually be to choose a plural form for the sentence subject and then use all the plural pronouns you like afterward.

The problem also arises in the following construction: "When a child becomes aggressive, they often need a nap." The author of this sentence has mixed up *a child* and *they* and has then gone on to compound the damage by allowing all these children only one nap. Are they sharing the same nap? Here are some ways out: "Naps often help when children have become aggressive." "When a child becomes aggressive, put that child to sleep for a nap." "When a child becomes aggressive, he or she needs a nap."

Exercise 5

Find some sentences with pronouns. Underline the pronoun and the noun to which it refers.

> *You'll find all you need in the final subsection of this article:* Jay, T. (2009). Do offensive words harm people? *Psychology, Public Policy, and Law, 15,* 81–101.

1. We isolated participants by placing them in cardboard boxes.

2. Freud emphasized the individual's need for soft drinks as well as his or her confrontation with sexuality.

3. _____

_____

_____

4. _____

_____

_____

Run-On Sentence or Comma Splice

To understand how to avoid run-on sentences, you will have to back up and understand once and for all what an independent clause is. A *clause* is a group of related words containing a subject and a predicate. An *independent clause* makes complete sense and is just like a sentence. A *dependent clause* also contains a subject and a predicate, but it begins with a word that ruins the whole prospect of looking like a sentence. It does not make complete sense because that little introductory word *depends* on another part of the sentence to make sense.

Independent clause: The participants ate the sausages.

Dependent clause: Although the participants ate the sausages

You may not join two independent clauses with a comma. (If you do, you have written a run-on sentence or a comma splice.) For example: "The participants ate the sausages, the experimenter watched." (Run-on sentence.)

To correct the situation, you have three choices: (1) make two sentences by trading the comma for a period; (2) trade the comma for a semicolon—after all, something made you think these two sentences felt like one; or (3) join the two with a *coordinating conjunction*. Put a comma before the conjunction. Memorize the list of coordinating conjunctions now:

    and   but   for   nor   or   so   yet   whereas

Getting back to the original problem, here are some solutions:

The participants ate the sausages; the experimenter watched.

The participants ate the sausages. The experimenter watched.

The participants ate the sausages, and the experimenter watched.

Exercise 6

Find some examples of sentences with two independent clauses joined by a coordinating conjunction.

You can find plenty of examples in the same section of the article that was suggested for Exercise 5.

1. We instructed participants to sit comfortably, yet no chairs were provided.

2. These results show no relationship between gender and hair length, but they support the results of previous studies.

3. _____

_____

4. _____

_____

   The other way to get into trouble with a run-on sentence is to join two independent clauses with the wrong kind of conjunctive word: a *conjunctive adverb.* Here is an example: "The participants ate the sausages, however, the experimenters never saw a thing." *However* is one of the words (conjunctive adverb) that cannot legally join two independent clauses. When you find one of these run-ons in your work, make two sentences out of it: "The participants ate the sausages. However, the experimenters never saw a thing." Put a comma after the conjunctive adverb.

   Here is a list of conjunctive adverbs that are likely to get you into this type of trouble:

afterward	also	besides	consequently
furthermore	however	indeed	later
likewise	moreover	nevertheless	otherwise
similarly	then	therefore	thus

   Notice what lovely words they are when they begin sentences. Use them whenever you can. Just do not use them to join two independent clauses.

Punctuation

Colons With Lists

Sometimes a colon introduces a list. Some students use a colon to introduce every list. However, if you have a word or phrase that indicates that a list is on its way, use a comma instead. These are some common examples:

for example   for instance   namely   that is

The exception to this rule is *as follows* or *the following*. These list-introducing phrases *do* take a colon. Another exception is *such as*. That one has *no* punctuation before the list.

Sometimes a list just serves as the object of a verb: "The participants touched turtles, snakes, lizards, and jellyfish." If you are inclined to put a colon after the word *touched* in that sentence, stop it.

If it sounds as if most lists need no colons, it sounds about right. The only really good time to use a colon (other than with *as follows*) is when an entire sentence (or independent clause) introduces the list. Do not use a colon after forms of the verb *to be* such as *is* or *are*.

Exercise 7

Find examples of colon usage with lists.

1. There were three conditions: turtle scenario, snake scenario, and lizard scenario.

2. The experimenter gave these instructions: Complete the questionnaire and draw a birthday cake on the back of each page.

3. _____

_____

4. _____

_____

Comma Before and (and Sometimes or)

Some students use a *mistaken* rule that looks like this: Use a comma before every *and* and, while you're at it, every *or*. This is probably the result of overlearning this rule: Use a comma before the *and* that coordinates two independent clauses (actually, before any of the coordinating conjunctions). Or this one: Use a comma before the *and* (and *or*) that signals the last item in a series.

But no comma is allowed before the *and* in the compound subject or compound predicate (unless there is a series longer than two—if
so, use the series rule for commas). Here is an example of this *error*:
"The participants read every fourth word, and ate every third olive." No
comma is allowed in that sentence—take it out: "The participants read
every fourth word and ate every third olive." That *and* simply joins the
two parts of a compound predicate. Without the distracting details, it
just says that they read and ate. You would never put a comma in if that
was all there was: "They read and ate."

The same goes for a compound subject: "The fourth-grade boys
with shoes, and the third-grade girls with hats traded insults." That
comma is illegal—take it out. It merely joins the two parts of a compound subject: "The boys and girls traded insults." When you think you
need a comma before a coordinating conjunction, find the bare bones
of the sentence—the single-word subject, verb, and object—and see
how the comma feels. If it still feels good, do it.

Exercise 8

Find sentences with very wordy compound subjects, predicates, and
objects. Notice that they do not have commas—unless the compound is
of three or more items, of course.

> ***There is an example here in the first paragraph:*** Lawson, A. E.
> (2002). The origin of conditional logic: Does a cheater detection
> module exist? *Journal of Genetic Psychology, 163,* 425–444.

1. This startling claim was supported by a statistical analysis that failed
   to find a significant direct relation between age and ability to dance
   the tango but did find significant relationships between age and a
   positive view of tango dancers and between a positive view of tango
   dancers and ability to tango.

2. This is assessed by a decrease in heart rate and/or an increase in
   vigilance in response to pushes and shoves as a consequence of
   prior exposure to pushes and shoves.

3. _____

   _____

   _____

Comma When You Need a Breath

It is easy to see why someone might be tempted to use a comma when sentence parts get very long: You need a breath. However, needing a breath is an absolutely illegal use of the comma. If that is the only reason you can think of, do not do it. Sometimes this mistake results in the placement of a comma between the subject and the predicate—something that no one would do on purpose.

Exercise 9

Read the sentences from the previous exercise aloud. Even though they have no commas, feel free to take a breath while saying them.

Important Differences Between People and Things

The relative pronoun *who* is for people. You may never use anything else. This sentence contains a common mistake: "The participants that were in the first group rode horses." If participants are people, use *who* instead of *that*.

Exercise 10

Find sentences with people referred to by the relative pronoun *who.*

You can go back to the same section of the same article suggested for Exercise 5 to find two examples.

1. Individuals who went to bed early were likely to wake up wealthier and wiser than those who went to bed late.
2. Participants who did not return for the second session were asked to clean the chalkboards.

3. _____

_____

4. _____

_____

Looking Back and Looking Ahead

If you look back, it would seem that you have finished. This chapter tidied up some grammar messes. You will be able to avoid fairly common pitfalls. Your constructions will now be parallel, and your reader will always know what is better than what. The parts of your sentences will agree with each other, and you will know what it means if a professor complains that they do not. Commas will not appear out of nowhere because they look nice. And your people will be referred to by the words *who* and *whom* rather than *that*.

So what can be left to do? Check the appendix for some hints on revising and proofreading. Finally, for those fortunate readers who are asked to present their research in a public forum, the next chapter provides some guidance for preparation of posters and PowerPoint presentations.

For more information:

Topic	Publication Manual	Concise Rules
Subject–verb agreement	3.19	1.19
Pronoun agreement	3.20	1.20
Comparisons	3.09	1.09
Parallel construction	3.23	1.23
Comma	4.03	2.03
Colon	4.05	2.05

CHAPTER *11*

Preparing a Presentation

Many students are required to prepare a research report in the style of an APA manuscript for at least one psychology class. However, because your first professional presentation of your research is more likely to be in the form of a poster presentation, many psychology departments are encouraging students to participate in poster sessions during their undergraduate years. In some cases, this is an in-house forum for advanced psychology majors; in others, it is a requirement of the Research Methods class. There are also several regional and national undergraduate research conferences every year that feature poster presentations by students in psychology and other sciences. In addition, many students present research at state and regional psychology conventions such as the Southeastern Psychological Association convention. Some of these have sessions sponsored by Psi Chi, the national honor society for psychology students, just for student posters. In addition to posters, students are increasingly being asked to present their research orally in PowerPoint presentations.

Poster Presentations

What Is a Poster Session?

Research is presented in the form of a display covering a board measuring about 4 by 6 feet. The boards are arranged in rows filling the room reserved for this purpose. It may be as large as a convention hall or as small as a classroom. You, the researcher, stand in front of your display, and interested people stop, read, chat, ask questions, or offer advice. This goes on for one to two hours.

Presenting a poster has advantages over presenting a talk. For one thing, it is less frightening. For another, only people who really have an interest in your work are stopping to look at it, and you have their full attention. You may come away with ideas for how to improve your next study or how the current data could be better presented. The observer can ask questions and spend as little or as much time with a presentation as he or she wants. The disadvantage is that it requires some serious planning to make the presentation as reader friendly as possible in this type of situation. People will be standing up, distracted by a lot of ambient noise, and unsure how much time to commit to any given poster in light of those that remain to be seen. If you develop strong empathy for the consumer's plight, it will help you to decide what to present on your poster and how to display it.

Even though poster presentations are becoming increasingly popular for disseminating research findings, the *Publication Manual* provides no guidance for preparing one. What, then, do authors rely on for poster rules? First, when a poster is accepted for presentation, presenters are usually given very brief guidelines from the organization sponsoring the conference. These generally include (1) the size of the display area each author will have, (2) the suggestion that the poster should be readable from a distance of about 3 feet (with the lettering for title, author, and affiliation at least 1 inch high and the rest at least 3.8 inches high), and (3) a diagram of possible arrangements of title, abstract, introduction, method, results, and conclusions.

▲ REMINDER BOX ▼
Your poster must be readable from a distance of 3 feet.

Although these are useful guidelines, the second method for learning how to present your findings in poster format is even more effective: Go to a poster session. You will see that there are limitless ways to follow the general rules conference organizers provide, and you may even see that some people have ignored the rules completely. You will quickly learn, for example, that the rule about the font being legible from a distance is not a good one to break because no one seems inclined to read the posters with small print. Students in or near major metropolitan areas might have the opportunity to attend a national or regional psychology meeting. If your university has an annual forum of some type, do not miss it. Or perhaps a neighboring university hosts conferences you can attend.

You are not bound by APA style—only by the spirit of the style. That means that you must be clear, fair to those whose work came before yours, and intellectually honest about the positive and negative sides of what you have done. But it also means that you do not need to follow a rigid format. You can use numbered lists or bulleted points instead of paragraphs, for example. You can use tables or circles and arrows to illustrate your theories or research design.

▲ REMINDER BOX ▼

Posters are true to the spirit of APA format, but the rules of presentation are relaxed.

Preparing the Poster

Use the same abstract that you prepared for your written research report. This is the only section that can remain unchanged.

The introduction will have to be very different from the one you used in the written report. You have to include the purpose and significance of your topic and your hypotheses, but you must reduce the literature review considerably. Here are some ways to highlight relevant literature:

■ Discuss the first study to address your topic in its current form. Then describe a very relevant recent one, especially if you are replicating and extending it. There might be more than one very similar to yours; mention several of the most similar.

■ Discuss the competing theoretical positions surrounding your work. Then describe the study that most closely resembles your method.

■ Provide a general explanation without references about how this problem has been addressed traditionally in research. Then explain, with references if appropriate, how you will diverge from this tradition and why.

Keep the introduction as short as you can. Try to keep it to two or three pages of large type. Remember the distractions that the reader faces. In these situations, people might read only a part of what you have written. If there is a crucial section of the introduction that you want to be sure gets read, make it visually distinct from the rest. Do this with the tricks your computer can produce: bullets, frames, bold italics, color.

▲ REMINDER BOX ▼

Make the introduction section no longer than three large-type pages.

The Method section has the potential to attract the most attention. Decide what is the most efficient way for someone to get the feeling of what the participants experienced. You might want to post the materials themselves (or some portions of them). If you showed pictures, post them. If participants read vignettes, put up a sample. If they performed a task with a piece of equipment, include a photograph of someone using the equipment. If they made copies of drawings, put up an example of the drawing and a sample copy. You do not have to provide the detail necessary to replicate, but you do have to provide the minimum necessary for someone to understand what you did. Of course, if you borrowed any of the details from a previous author, you should provide the references. In a brief narrative of the procedure, include enough to satisfy the reader that you did it right. That is, provide:

■ The number of participants and any important data about them

■ The design

■ A brief description of the task

■ The grouping variables

■ The nature of the control condition

▲ REMINDER BOX ▼

Consider posting parts or photos of the actual materials.

The results you post will be primarily tables and figures. Use color; be creative. You can even use little icons or clip art to label the parts (e.g., lines on a line graph) instead of a legend. (Don't go crazy here—your purpose is instant recognition of the variable, not an award for funniest poster.) You need only introduce your visual displays with a statement of the analyses you conducted and the significant findings. Try to keep all the words (e.g., label of y-axis) horizontal.

Instead of a discussion, posters usually have *conclusions.* The difference is that conclusions are less speculative and more directly tied to the hypotheses and results. There is no room for implications or suggestions for future research. Conclusions can be a few numbered points that you make about the relationship between the results and the hypotheses.

▲ REMINDER BOX ▼

Posters usually have conclusions instead of discussion.

You will have to prepare a References section if you referred to others' work. Occasionally, you will see posters without references, but students should plan on a brief list of references.

Typically, posters are prepared using a program such as Power-Point and then printed on a single sheet with a large-format printer. You set up a single PowerPoint slide sized to match the requirements specified by the conference organizers (e.g., 24 × 36 in. or 36 × 48 in.). If you do not have the use of such a printer, you can find online services or local businesses that do the printing. It is costly but necessary.

Remember that the poster should be readable from about 3 ft. Find a font size that will do this by working at 100% view in your word processor and trying out a few fonts. Then step back. Some fonts work well in bold typeface throughout. Others are already bold enough when printed in very large size. Section titles can be set apart by color and font size. Many people use their university logo somewhere on the poster. You can probably find one designed for sharing somewhere on your university's website. But don't feel compelled to do this. It's a matter of personal taste unless your school has a policy on it.

If you do not already know how, you need to learn how to manage text boxes for this task. Place each element of your presentation (e.g., abstract) in its own text box and line them up—across or down—in a way that makes the flow obvious. Use numbers or arrows if it is not obvious. Make the titles of these sections large and clear. Copy and paste the material from your word-processed draft. Keep it brief. Leave a lot of white space. Keep the background light (white is lovely) rather than use a lot of color and texture in the background. There are many templates on the web that you can hunt through. They are not all excellent, however. And if you are purchasing the printing through an online service, many of them offer templates as well. Purrington (2009) has a great site at http://www.swarthmore.edu/NatSci/cpurrin1/posteradvice .htm—even though he is a biologist! (Some of his advice doesn't apply to you, though; for example, he suggests that a poster should not contain an abstract, but that is contrary to our cultural environment.) He also sponsors a "Pimp My Poster" group on Flickr: http://www.flickr .com/groups/688685@N24/ where people post their drafts and get advice. Here are two additional sites with templates that I found in an Internet search:

> www.sacs.ucsf.edu/Newsletters/Templates/36x48_horiz _template.ppt

> http://groups.ucanr.org/posters/Templates_for_Posters/

The second one has a useful example of scientific style—see if you can locate it among the various examples provided for other purposes on that website.

The take-home message for posters is that they need to be attractive enough for someone to pause and read, easy enough to read and understand in a noisy, busy environment (sometimes even with a cash bar nearby), and assembled in a way that puts science ahead of everything else.

Finally, print a copy of the poster on your own printer. Use the "scale fit to paper" command. You'll get a good idea of the clarity of your presentation. If you can't read it without a magnifying glass, your font is too small. (You will be able to use this reduced version as a handout at the conference.) Make sure that your e-mail address is on the poster, and if it is too small to be legible on the handout, prepare a version with an enlarged e-mail address just for the handout.

▲ REMINDER BOX ▼

Don't value artiness or cuteness above science, but don't ignore it either.

Preparing Yourself

What will actually happen at the poster session is that strangers will walk up to your poster, give it a glance, and do one of three things:

1. Walk away.
2. Read it.
3. Talk to you.

If they walk away, you will feel rejected. No one can adequately prepare for that. But be aware that people have different interests, and the topic of your poster is not on everyone's "A list." If they read it, you will wonder what to do with yourself while this is happening. Again, until it happens, you cannot know how to prepare. But if they talk to you, you *can* be prepared. That is because they always say approximately the same thing: "Tell me the quick version of what you did." You went to all the trouble of making it artistic, easy to read, and self-standing. Yet this lazy stranger wants you to tell about it? Shocking! But you can be ready with the speech you have prepared. Go for the visual space that you have designed to stand out—point to it and give your already prepared quick oral version. If this is an in-house event or an undergraduate meeting for the sciences in general, you might have nonpsychologists in attendance. Prepare a version in lay terms. If this is a professional meeting for psychologists, prepare a version intended for general psychologists.

Finally, here is advice from my own Research Methods class. After the students presented posters for the first time, I asked what would be the single most important piece of advice they would give to next year's class. Their answer? Eat lunch first and wear comfortable shoes!

Oral Presentations

PowerPoint presentation software is a good organizing tool for public speaking. However, students and professionals have been known to overuse some of its features. If you are preparing to present your research to a group—in a class or at a conference—remember that the most important object in the room is *you*, not the screen. People should be involved with what you are saying, not with what you have on a board behind you. A few simple rules will help you to arrange that.

About You

- Practice. Try to be able to speak without looking at notes. Have them in your hand or on the podium, but just so that you will sleep better the night before, not so that you can be less prepared when the time comes. Know when to change slides and know how to do it on the equipment you will have. Get there early enough to understand how the machines work in that room.

- Be prepared for equipment failure. Be able to talk without the slides.

- Dress professionally. If your classroom attire is casual, kick it up a notch on the day of your talk. Notice that at a conference, the speakers are usually dressed more professionally than many in the audience.

- Look at your audience, not at your slides. To make eye contact, you have to be looking at something with eyes. So does your audience.

The Content of Your Slides

Use the slides to outline your talk. Use phrases and isolated words onscreen, and elaborate in your talk on the basis of what is on the screen. Never put complete sentences on your slides, and you will not be very tempted to read the slides. You can put material on slides that is important but boring, such as the demographic data describing your participants. A slide can show the total number, their gender breakdown, and their ages, and you can say something different—more interesting—about them (perhaps that they were all prisoners or all single parents) and then just stand for a moment so that your audience can take in the numbers on the screen.

Strive for clarity of form and content. Use simple fonts and make them bold. Remember that less is more; make only a few points with each slide. Most experienced presenters recommend no more than six lines of text and no more than six words per line. Another common guideline is that a 20-minute presentation should have no more than 20 slides.

You can cite references, but just the author and year. It is not necessary to put the full reference on your slide. People will find the source if they need it. Do not read the year of publication aloud. Finally, do not put up a reference list at the end.

Tables and graphs are very welcome. But do *not* read the numbers. Discuss the trends. For example, you can put a means table up, and without reading the numbers, you can indicate which means were significantly different. You can put up a correlation table and call attention to significant relationships—again, without stating numbers that are there for all to see. For graphs, make sure the labels are large enough for the audience to read. If you use a graph, refer to the colors to describe the trends:

> The red bars reflect the time spent on homework, and the blue bars reflect time spent in paid employment. The first pair of bars represents the athletes, and the second pair represents the cheerleaders. As you see, both groups spent little time in paid employment (and that small difference on the graph is not significant), but the cheerleaders spent much more time watching television.

After describing your method (some sample items from measures would be welcome on screen), you can combine talk of hypotheses, results, and discussion. That is, you can say that you expected a certain outcome. Then show the graph or table that resulted. Say a few interesting discussion-type things about it. Then move on to your next hypothesis. Nothing will be lost if you fail to use headings for results and discussion.

Another thing that you can do is work with symbols. Any symbolic representations of your data or your ideas will also enhance your posters, by the way. Here are some examples:

> Use horizontal arrows when you want to imply time sequence or causation:

> > Ice cream cones to participants → higher return rate for questionnaires

> > Electric shock → lower return rate

> Use vertical arrows for *up* and *down*, for example when you want to say which groups improved and which did not:

> > Depression   older adults ↑ younger adults ↓
> > Anxiety   older adults ↑ younger adults ↓
> > Life satisfaction   older adults ↑ younger adults ↑

> Use greater than (>), less than (<), or equal (=) signs to show group differences:

> > Hypothesis 1: depression

> > > older adults > younger adults

Hypothesis 2: life satisfaction

older adults < younger adults

Avoid Distracting Effects

Avoid the following distractions:

- Images that are decorative rather than explanatory
- Weird fonts (Arial and Verdana are always safe)
- Small fonts
- Fonts that change from slide to slide
- Animation and flying text
- Text moving in from different places for each slide
- Too many colors
- Annoying color contrast—use high contrasting colors (a safe choice would be a white or very light background with a black or blue font)
- Busy backgrounds
- Backgrounds that change from one slide to the next

Looking Back and Looking Ahead

In addition to presenting your work in written format, you are now prepared to make a poster or oral presentation. Often, the poster presentation is done as a first step in making your findings public. It is easy to submit to a conference if you have good data; the rules for submission generally require a short summary. If you are submitting a poster, you just need to prepare the broad outlines and a few details. While you are attending your poster presentation, you might get some good ideas for further analysis or further research.

At many conferences, the oral presentations are reserved for more complete projects, and they are often part of a group of presentations on a similar topic—a symposium. The symposium is the conference submission, and if it is accepted, all of the talks are included as a package. However, students are often required to practice all the formats for presenting research.

Now that you have come to the end of this book, you are ready to show off your skills, no matter what the venue.

Wrapping It Up

You are probably not surprised to learn that after you have written the first draft of your paper, you still have work to do. But the worst is over, so give yourself a moment to enjoy that feeling. I have called this section of the book "Wrapping It Up" because the phrase has two meanings. Think of the rewriting and editing you do after the first draft in two ways: (a) You will now finish up your project, and (b) you will do what is necessary to make it an appealing package.

Students sometimes call this job *proofreading,* but that is not the correct word. It makes it sound as though after your first draft, all you have to do is check it over for typos and spelling errors. That is what you do with the last draft, which is a bit farther down the line. *First, you revise; second, you edit; third, you proofread.* Each of these may involve more than one draft.

First Rewrite

The first rewrite (resulting in the second draft) must be conceptual. This will be a long process, so save a day to do it. The best idea is to finish your first draft two full days before it is due (assuming that you can devote a big part of those two days to this paper—otherwise, allow extra days). In this rewrite, you will not give style a thought.

Introduction

Think through your sequencing of paragraphs. Try to remember what your purpose was for each one, and now review the order to see whether it is correct. Make sure you have all the pieces of your argument in place. Check to make sure that you have included the following:

■ The purpose of your study

■ Why it is important

■ Hypotheses or research questions

■ Rationales for hypotheses

■ General information about method

■ Definitions of variables

Look for paragraphs with only one or two sentences. If you find any, fix them now. Elaborate on what you have written, move the material to a more logical place, or remove those sentences.

Now try to outline your paper. Outline what is really there, not what you meant to write. Step back and see whether that outline is the best possible organization of your source material. If you see whole paragraphs in the wrong place, move them. After they have been moved, make sure transitions still work, or change them. If you find gaps where something should be explained or fleshed out, do it.

Check your subheadings. See if they still work now that you have made some changes. Can you improve on them? If you have not used subheadings, consider putting some in now.

Method

First, look over your subheadings and confirm that they accurately describe the material in each section. Next, examine the information that you provide about participants. Check to make sure that you have reported the following:

■ Age and gender

■ Type of population they represent (e.g., first-year psychology students)

- Compensation they received for participating
- The number of those who did not complete the study and why
- Appropriate demographic information for each group (if applicable)
- Statistical power

Look at the *procedure.* Try very hard to put yourself in the shoes of someone who was not there. Are there any sentences that would not make sense for that person? If so, they are not necessarily bad sentences; more likely, they are in the wrong place. The best thing would be to try this section out on a friend. As you read it aloud, watch that person's face. If you notice a funny look, you have skipped some information that someone needs in order to put the pieces together clearly. Alternatively, have the friend read the section aloud to you.

Check to make sure that you have

- Done a good job conveying the instructions you gave to participants
- Provided enough information to replicate
- Included instructions on scoring (if applicable)

If you used an *apparatus,* check to make sure that you

- Provided enough information for replication
- Made clear the experience participants had while using it
- Indicated how someone could buy or build it

If you have a special section for *materials,* does it stand alone or does it depend on information about conditions? If it makes no sense to someone who is as yet unfamiliar with your conditions, reorganize now. If you have used materials created by someone else, check to make sure that you have included the appropriate reference. If you have created your own materials, have you provided examples? Is there enough information to replicate?

Results

Look at your original data analysis. Make sure that every analysis that should be in your paper is there. Double-check *every* number against the printout from the statistics package you used or against the math that you did. This is also a good time to make sure that letters used in reporting statistics (e.g., *t, n, F, p*) are italicized (but do not italicize the Greek letters).

If you have used tables or figures to display data, every one of them should be mentioned in this section. There should be enough information in the text to allow the reader to know what types of data are in the tables and figures. Also, the relevant means and percentages should be either in the text or in tables (or figures) but not in both places.

Discussion

With your introduction on one side and your discussion on the other, check to make sure that every hypothesis or question mentioned in one is mentioned in the other. Next, with your results on one side and your discussion on the other, do the same thing.

Now outline your Discussion section. If you have only topics and no subtopics in your outline, you might have restated your results without discussing them. Remember your options:

- Similarities between your findings and someone else's

- Differences between your findings and someone else's

- Relationship between these findings and theories mentioned in your introduction

- Alternative explanations for the findings

- Suggested explanations for negative results

- Limitations of the study

- Implications of the findings

- Practical applications

- Suggestions for further research (with rationales)

References

This is a good time to check your references. Every reference in your paper should be in your References list and vice versa. Check the spellings while you are at it; your spelling-checker will not pick up errors in people's names.

Abstract

The last part of the first rewrite is checking the abstract. Assuming that you worked pretty hard to get it right the first time, you have only to double-check at this point to make sure that any changes you have made in the body of the paper do not affect the abstract. If you are still happy with the abstract, move on to the next part of the wrap-up.

Second Rewrite

With your major revisions behind you, it is time to concentrate on style. Now you will see whether you can tighten up your organization at the paragraph level and make sure your sentences are clean.

Begin with the paragraphs. Does each one start with a topic sentence? Is there something about that sentence that makes it clear why the paragraph is located where it is? For example, is there a subheading nearby that makes the reader expect such a topic? Is there a transition word that relates to the previous paragraph? Remember, you have a list in Chapter 2—use it. Finally, does every sentence in that paragraph relate to the topic?

You are probably sick of the paper by now, but that is to be expected. You will learn to love this paper again before you hand it in because it will be a really attractive package. After all, you have just put on the wrapping paper and taped it closed. Still, some of the tape might be missing, and you have not tied it up in a ribbon yet.

Now you have to check every sentence for gross errors. First, make sure each sentence is really a sentence—not a run-on or a fragment. Next, find the grammatical subject of every sentence and underline it. Then, make sure the verb is appropriate in number. While you are at it, make sure the verb defines an action that is logically possible for the subject. For example, if you have written that an experiment *tried* to do something, now is the time to reconsider. Think about misplaced modifiers at this time. Admittedly, misplaced modifiers are not easy to spot in one's own work, but sometimes when you are studying your sentences this closely, you can spot them.

This is also the time to check for errors in parallel construction. These, too, can be hard to spot; look especially at items in a series, compound verbs, and phrases containing comparisons.

Now your package is securely covered in paper that will not come off. No untrimmed edges are showing.

Third Inspection—Not a Rewrite

You are nearing the home stretch—preparing to put a ribbon on that package. Pass your eyes over your paper again. Circle the commas and colons. Try to remind yourself of the rule you learned in school or in this book that prescribes that punctuation mark in that place. You should have a grammar book somewhere on your desk; perhaps you can find that rule. If you cannot specify the rule, you should seriously consider omitting the punctuation mark. Most of what is left can be streamlined with the use of the search function on your word processor. If you are not yet familiar with this function, take some time now to figure out how to *find* or *search* for a word or phrase. Also, it is a good idea to figure out the command that takes you to the top of your document because it will be efficient to return there after each search. When you are ready, search and correct if necessary:

- *Apostrophe:* For each one, if it is used in a contraction, change the contraction to a more formal phrase. If it is a simple plural with no possession intended, omit the apostrophe. If the intention is possessive but the word is a pronoun, omit the apostrophe. If it is a possessive noun, note whether it is singular or plural and make sure the apostrophe is in the right place.

- *Their:* First, make sure you didn't mean to write *there.* When that is taken care of, check to make sure that the noun referred to is apparent to the reader and that it is plural. Then do a search for *there* just to make sure you did not mean to write *their.*

- *Feel, felt, think, thought, believe, believed, said, state, stated, prove,* and *proved:* If these refer to the activities of researchers you have cited, think it over. Perhaps you should substitute one of the words on your list of researcher verbs in Chapter 2.

- *Current* and *present:* Do not use these words to refer to experiments other than yours.

- *Data, hypotheses, hypothesis, stimulus, stimuli, analysis, analyses, phenomena, phenomenon, criteria,* and *criterion:* There is always a danger that the verbs in these sentences might not agree in number with these nouns.

- *Since* and *while:* Remember, the *Publication Manual* specifies that these words are used only in their temporal sense. You might need to substitute *because* and *whereas* if they are more accurate.

- *Between* and *among:* Use *between* for two things, *among* for more than two.

- *You* and *we:* Unless you are quoting instructions to participants, rephrase without these words.

- *Quotation marks:* Try one more time to paraphrase instead of quote.

- *Non, pre, post,* and *sub:* These are not words. They have to be attached to other words.

- *Ampersands* (&) should appear only in parentheses and in the References section. Authors' names are joined by *and* outside of parentheses.

- *Latin abbreviations:* Make sure they are punctuated correctly and that they appear only in parentheses. See the final section of Chapter 2 if you need a refresher.

Now you can run your spell-checker. It will not help you with names, so look them over each time the spell-checker finds them. Check the spelling yourself.

Final Touches

You have only one task left. Read your paper aloud. Read every word you have written. This is the way you will notice whether you have left little words out or put extra ones in. All writers have trouble seeing dumb little mistakes because they know what something is supposed to say. Cognitive psychologists call this *top-down processing*. Our minds are working with meaning, and sometimes our eyes miss the details.

This is the time when you begin to feel proud of your work; you are not feeling as sick of it as you were by the second revision. This is because you can appreciate how many little improvements you made even after you thought you were finished. You can finally take this paper out in public (or hand it in to your professor), and it will surely make a good impression.

References

American Psychological Association. (2010a). *Concise rules of APA style* (6th ed.). Washington, DC: Author.

American Psychological Association. (2010b). *Publication manual of the American Psychological Association* (6th ed.). Washington, DC: Author.

Bem, D. J. (1995). Writing a review article for *Psychological Bulletin. Psychological Bulletin, 118,* 172–177.

Nicol, A. A. M., & Pexman, P. M. (1999). *Presenting your findings: A practical guide for creating tables.* Washington, DC: American Psychological Association.

Nicol, A. A. M., & Pexman, P. M. (2003). *Displaying your findings: A practical guide for creating figures, posters, and presentations.* Washington, DC: American Psychological Association.

Purrington, C. B. (2009). Advice on designing scientific posters. Retrieved from http://www.swarthmore.edu/NatSci/cpurrin1/posteradvice.htm

Rimer, S. (2003, September 3). A campus fad that's being copied: Internet plagiarism seems on the rise. Retrieved from http://select .nytimes.com/search/restricted/article?res=F60F10F9395C0C708 CDDA00894DB404482

Talab, R. S. (2000). Copyright, plagiarism, and Internet-based research projects: Three "golden rules." *Tech Trends, 44*(4), 7–9.

Index